A
History
of the
International Anglican
Liturgical Consultations
(IALCs)
1983-2007

by
David Holeton

Canadian Anglican Presbyter,
Professor of Liturgy at the Charles University in Prague

and
Colin Buchanan

English Anglican Bishop, Retired

Contents

THE COVER PICTURE
is the Compass Rose, symbol of the Anglican Communion,
reproduced here by permission of the Anglican Communion Office.

First Impression June 2007

ISSN 0951-2667
ISBN 978-1-85311-843-2

Introduction

For more than twenty years, the International Anglican Liturgical Consultations (IALCs) have not just occupied a corner in the history of the Anglican Communion, but have also become a live part of the Communion's systems of international communication and co-ordination. We write to chart that development and put the major characteristics of the Consultations thus far on record. We do so, acknowledging that our only distinctive qualification for writing this account is that we are the only two persons with an unbroken record of attendance at the Consultations; however we also were known by the Alcuin/GROW Joint Editorial Board, when they commissioned us, to have a keen interest in getting such an account into print, as we have shared with each other a concern, as generations start to pass on, that a firsthand account should be written while it can be.

We are deeply indebted to the labours of many who have given help, but most notably the following:

Donald Gray, who as Rector of Liverpool and chair of the British Joint Liturgical Group shared in the original convening, and later, as Canon of Westminster, hosted a crucial London meeting.

Paul Gibson of Canada, who in 1989 was seconded by his own Church to the Anglican Consultative Council to become the ACC Co-ordinator for Liturgy. In this capacity he became honorary secretary and administrator to the IALCs, and, continuing as such beyond his formal retirement in 1999, he retains the role to the present day. His labours were recognized by the Archbishop of Canterbury's award of the Cross of St Augustine in October 2006.[1]

Ronald Dowling, incumbent over the years of three parishes in different parts of Australia, who had ten years on the Steering Committee, including six as chair, and was at the centre of a notable incident recorded in chapter 11.

---

[1]   There are regular contributions by Paul Gibson in the ACC reports from 1990 to 2002, and these contain information about IALCs, and are noted in passing in the chapters below. He also wrote an account of IALCs for the 1998 Lambeth Conference, but the official report did not include it, and he then retouched it slightly for publication as 'International Anglican Liturgical Consultations: A Review' in *Studia Liturgica* Vol.XXIX (1999). For the years until 1997 his account gives a somewhat fuller picture of the theological content of each Statement than the present overall history is able to do.

Paul Bradshaw, perhaps the Anglican world's leading academic liturgist at the time of writing, who became chair of the Steering Committee in 2001, and continues to lead it until the end of the Palermo Consultation in July-August 2007.

In addition, Deirdre Martin (neé Hoban, see page 13) of the Anglican Consultative Council (ACC) office hunted through the archives of the ACC and made them available to us to provide accurate documentation, and Colin James, Colin Craston, Bill Crockett, and Trevor Lloyd have also assisted with written documentation or recollections.

The whole IALC enterprise has been much helped by the readiness of the Alcuin/GROW Joint Editorial Board, and of Grove Books Ltd, the Anglican Book Centre, Toronto, and Columba Books, Dublin, to publish our work. At the time of writing these publications are, with one exception, still in print, mostly in two formats, one of simply the particular Statement and the other of a fuller volume including essays and other documentation.[2] There has been real encouragement in the sale of these publications, and particularly in the evidence of individual provinces engaged in liturgical revision turning to the work of IALCs for their guidance and criteria.[3] We look to the Lambeth Conference of 2008, amid all its potentially distracting agenda, to give a stamp of approval to the Consultations, and, where the bishops are discussing liturgy, full weight to the successive Statements. It would be a long step forward from the oddities of the last two Lambeth Conferences if these considered liturgical principles, produced by the IALCs, were provided in advance for due scrutiny by members of any Section of the Conference which is likely to address liturgical issues.

While there are no doubt many valuable historical details which we have inadvertently omitted, we are fully aware that we have said nothing about worship at Consultations and Conferences. Let readers be assured that all the world has made its contributions, and that all the work of lectures, debates, group discussion, and drafting has been undertaken within a framework of regular ordered international worship of Almighty God.

David Holeton and Colin Buchanan
Easter Day 2007

[2] The exception is the original Boston Statement of 1985. See page 14 below.
[3] Thus we have reason to believe that the impact of the Boston and Toronto Statements on the admission of children to communion has been very weighty throughout the world, that the issue of true inculturation of the liturgy has been greatly furthered by the York Statement, that the Dublin Statement has been studied in most provinces revising eucharistic liturgies since 1995, and that the Churches of Ireland and England have both drawn confidently upon the Berkeley Statement in their new ordination rites of 2004 and 2005 respectively.

1. The Book of Common Prayer and the Liturgical Background of the Anglican Communion

For hundreds of years after the Reformation, Anglicans around the world had but a single notion of 'The Book of Common Prayer'. There were variants from 1662 around – the Scottish eucharistic tradition from the mid-18th century, and a complete American Book of Common Prayer from 1789 – but they were so clearly simply minor variants on the Anglican liturgical tradition, that they did not call into question what the concept of a 'BCP' might be. No doubt, as steamship and railway helped the world to shrink in the second half of the 19th century, more scope for comparisons came to exist; but in general Anglicans not only took their existing Prayer Book with them when they travelled the world, but they also defined themselves by their adherence to it, and built it into new diocesan and provincial constitutions.

The Anglican Communion became an international institution itself by virtue of the first Lambeth Conference in 1867 – and the BCP continued as a bond within the institution. The 1897 and 1908 Lambeth Conferences, though they have a worldwide purview, both cite 'The Book of Common Prayer' as though it were a known single entity (as indeed it very nearly was). The 1908 Resolution 36 provides just a glimpse of a possibly different future:

> 'While maintaining the authority of the Book of Common Prayer as the Anglican standard of doctrine and practice, we consider that liturgical uniformity should not be regarded as a necessity throughout the Anglican Communion.'

At that time there existed (apart from the Scottish liturgy) the American BCP (revised in 1892), and the Irish Book of 1878 (only a millimetre distant from 1662), and that was all. The 20th century, however, did see other revisions – a complete Book in Scotland in 1912 (and revised in 1929), an Irish-type revision in Canada in 1922, and a sprinkling of new eucharistic rites in East and Central Africa, South Africa, Korea, Japan, India, Ceylon, and elsewhere. These tended to diverge from 1662 not through any policy of inculturation, but simply on grounds of churchmanship. With the Scottish and American precedents already in existence, it became a norm for more catholic provinces to seek to restore to the eucharist 'the long prayer' – ie a 'canon' which ran as a single whole from sursum corda onwards, including preface, sanctus, a link to the narrative of institution, the narrative itself (usually with indented rubrics for manual acts), anamnesis, epiclesis (not invariable, as too 'eastern' for some provinces), self-oblation and/or petition for fruitful reception, doxology and 'amen'. Most other services in new BCPs remained close in their wording to 1662 – and in provinces where a catholic revising thrust was not to the fore, there 1662 itself continued, not through mere inertia, but as being both 'incomparable' as liturgy, and the authentic mark of being Anglican. The relatively standard character of the BCP worldwide is neatly attested as late as 1948 in Resolution 78(a) of the Lambeth Conference that year:

> 'The Conference holds that the Book of Common Prayer has been, and is, so strong a bond of unity throughout the Anglican Communion that great care must be taken to ensure that revisions of the Book shall be in accordance with the doctrine and accepted liturgical worship of the Anglican Communion.'

The last new Books produced on the old basis were the 1960 Book of the Church of India, Pakistan, Burma and Ceylon, and the 1962 Book of the Anglican Church in Canada. Both took their genesis from early in the 1950s, and became obsolete almost as soon as they were authorized. A whole series of new influences was reshaping the worship of the Communion. The following have been of particular weight:

1. The coming of the Liturgical Movement, and the bringing of the corporate sharing in communion into a central place in the life of many provinces (along with a reordering of the interiors of Gothic buildings, the beginnings of 'Westward position' for the president, and the slowly growing role of laypersons, in the ministry of the word, the intercessions, and the distribution of communion).

2. The provision in the united Church of South India of first the eucharistic liturgy in 1950, and then a complete *Book of Common Worship* in 1963, showing considerable independence from the Anglican BCP.

3. The findings of the subcommittee on liturgical revision at Lambeth 1958, which positively encouraged provincial liberty to revise texts and provide for local needs.[4]

---

[4] *The Lambeth Conference 1958* (SPCK, 1958) 2.78-98. Resolution 74 commended the report, though Resolution 73 had whistled to keep up its pan-Anglican courage with the frankly utopian welcoming of 'the contemporary movement towards unanimity in doctrinal and liturgical matters by those of differing traditions in the Anglican Communion as a result of new knowledge gained from Biblical and liturgical studies'.

4. The impact of Vatican II (1962-65) and the consequent worldwide radical changes in Roman Catholic liturgy and liturgical thinking. From this came unprecedented ecumenical co-operation, which, as will appear, helped precipitate the Anglican story told here.

5. The change in English-language address to God from 'thou' to 'you', a change precipitated by several factors, including modern versions of the Bible, actual changes by Rome, and a mood of informalizing derived from the Liturgical Movement. From 1966 onwards this led to a rewriting of almost all English-language liturgical texts, and brought international interdenominational agencies into the field.

2. Anglican Communion Consultations and Inter-action on Liturgy in the 1960s and 1970s

Lambeth 1958 showed some awareness of the forces they had unchained. The subcommittee recommended that a committee representative of the whole Communion should address the structure of the eucharist. This became resolution 76 of the whole Conference as follows:

'76. The Conference requests the Archbishop of Canterbury, in co-operation with the [Lambeth] Consultative Body, to appoint an Advisory Committee to prepare recommendations for the structure of the Holy Communion service which could be taken into consideration by any Church or Province revising its Eucharistic rite, and which would conserve the doctrinal balance of the Anglican tradition and take account of present liturgical knowledge.'

The wording of this reveals how the powers now lay: any province might diverge from the Prayer Book tradition, and no supra-provincial power existed to restrain it; so the bishops, knowing these limitations, were asking for a group to advise and recommend.

Archbishop Fisher seems simply to have passed the task in 1959 to the first Executive Officer of the Anglican Communion, Stephen Bayne, who himself was appointed as an outcome of resolution 61. It clearly did not rank high on his agenda, but a separate initiative in Africa relieved him of much need to be proactive. In Kampala, Uganda, in April 1961 there began a venture to compile a 'Liturgy for Africa', in which the metropolitans of the now five independent provinces in Africa would co-operate – that is, West Africa, East Africa, Central Africa, South Africa, and (newly formed that April) Uganda, Rwanda and Burundi. Leslie Brown, the host Archbishop, who had previously been secretary of both the CSI Liturgy Committee in 1948-52, and the 1958 Lambeth subcommittee on liturgy, was co-ordinator of the project.[5] An early draft of his came onto Stephen Bayne's desk, and he circulated it (with a sense of relief) in January 1962 to all the metropolitans of the Communion, and also to their designated 'correspondents' on liturgy, from a list he was compiling to have available in his office.[6] He apparently hoped that a draft actual liturgy would provide more useful guidance than an abstract outline structure. However, he also conceived the idea, as he planned for the pan-Anglican Congress at Toronto in 1963, to convene a smaller Liturgical Consultation from the participants there, to follow on immediately after

---

[5]   See L.W.Brown, *Relevant Liturgy* (OUP, 1965).

[6]   S.J. Bayne, *An Anglican Turning Point* (Church Historical Society, Austin, Texas, 1964) pp.19-20.

the Congress. This duly occurred and, quite apart from the discussion there of *A Liturgy for Africa*, the Consultation asked four persons to form a subcommittee to address the Lambeth Conference request for a document on the structure of a eucharistic liturgy.[7] The subcommittee included Leslie Brown (of course), Howard Clarke, the Primate of Canada, Bishop Kenneth Sansbury of Singapore[8], and Massey H.Shepherd, Jr (the leading PECUSA liturgist). Working by correspondence they produced their document (signed in the first person singular by Leslie Brown) and sent it to Stephen Bayne in July 1964. It was presented to the Archbishop of Canterbury, and, at his direction, sent out by Stephen Bayne's successor, Ralph Dean, early in 1965 to the metropolitans and the 'Liturgical Correspondents'. It is descriptive of a structure (for it could not be prescriptive) and is less than 1,000 words in total. It goes a long way towards the pattern of the eucharist that has since developed round the Communion.[9] In some provinces it was noted and even followed, in others it was noted, and in others again it was not noted.

While Lambeth 1968 did not address liturgical revision directly, it did have before it a report on revision around the Communion and met at a time when the process was quickening in a radical way all over the Communion.[10] In Resolution 25 it did address some issues of Christian initiation[11]:

> 'The Conference recommends that each province or regional church
> be asked to explore the theology of baptism and confirmation in
> relation to the need to commission the laity for their task in the
> world, and to experiment in this regard.'

History then repeated itself, as another Liturgical Consultation was convened to follow the 1968 Lambeth Conference. This post-Lambeth Consultation of about 30 persons, mostly bishops, asked Leslie Brown and Ronald Jasper to produce a revised version of the Pan-Anglican Document,

---

[7] See Colin Buchanan (ed) *Modern Anglican Liturgies 1958-1968* (OUP, 1968) pp.23-32 and 48-56. Roger Beckwith, in the chapter on the Pan-Anglican Document, points out that neither the Archbishop of Canterbury nor the Lambeth Consultative Body seems to have had any say in this forming of a subcommittee.

[8] Kenneth Sansbury wrote two essays on 'Revisions of the Eucharistic Rite in the Anglican Communion' in *Theology* in April and May 1954.

[9] The text of the Pan-Anglican Document is to be found as an appendix to *Prayer Book Studies XVII* (Church Pension Fund, NY, 1966) pp.58-59, and in Buchanan, *op.cit.* pp.31-32.

[10] The report was a compilation by Robert Jeffery on 'Liturgical Revision in the Anglican Communion since 1958' in *Lambeth Conference 1968: Preparatory Information* (SPCK, 1968) pp.35-70.

[11] A committee on 'Laymen and Laywomen' in Section II ('The Renewal of the Church in Ministry'), while seeking a 'commissioning of laymen analogous to the ordination of clergy', commended 'the following alternatives as possible lines of experiment:
   (a) Admission to Holy Communion and confirmation would be separated [admission coming first]...
   (b) Infant baptism and confirmation would be administered together, followed by admission to Holy Communion at an early age...' (*The Lambeth Conference 1968: Resolutions and Reports*, p.99) It is likely that this committee's report, including the oddity that people are first lay Christians and are then commissioned for their lay ministry, lies behind Resolution 25 reprinted above.

and to incorporate into it provision for the daily office also. They did this within months, and then published and circulated a somewhat fuller document with a 700-word introduction, *The Structure and Contents of the Eucharistic Liturgy and the Daily Office.*[12] The Liturgical Consultation also took note of the coming of modern English (the Document duly mentioned the International Consultation on English Texts – ICET), was interested in simplifying the calendar, and was frankly puzzled about supplementary consecration (asking for further study).

After 1968, the Anglican Communion itself took on an altered structure. At the request of the Lambeth Conference there was formed the Anglican Consultative Council (ACC), with a Secretary-General replacing the Executive Officer. The ACC first met in Limuru, near Nairobi, in 1971. Liturgy was not on its main agenda, but it passed a resolution as follows:

'26 *Liason between Liturgical Commissions*

Having received a request from the Liturgical Commission of the Church of England in Australia for the setting up of a Consultative Liturgical Committee, the Council recommends that the Secretary-General:

(a)   provide liaison between the Liturgical Commissions in the various Provinces of the Anglican Communion;

(b)   arrange for a report on liturgical matters to be made to the Anglican Consultative Council in 1973.'

Colin Buchanan commented 'It will be clear that the first of these recommendations falls far short of the recorded request from the Australian Liturgical Commission, and in effect leaves the Secretary-General's responsibilities exactly as they were before.'[13] It was, perhaps, hardly surprising – the ACC was only just establishing its identity and from the start was tightly squeezed financially. Only a major triumph of imagination and corporate will could have brought such a Committee into existence with any credibility.

The second part of resolution 26 was faithfully fulfilled, as the Secretary-General asked Ronald Jasper to compile a report 'Liturgy 1968-1973' for that next ACC meeting in Dublin. This reprinted the revised Pan-Anglican Structure Document and had brief paragraphs from most Anglican provinces, with more extended ones from England, Wales and the USA.[14] The Council agenda did not address liturgy, save for a paragraph noting a concern about initiation (with its focus on the shifting status and significance of confirmation) around the Communion. It asked the Secretary-General to circulate information about initiation to the member Churches.

---

[12]   The text is reprinted in Colin Buchanan (ed), *Further Anglican Liturgies 1968-1975* (Grove, Bramcote, 1975) pp.27-31 and in ACC, *Partners in Mission* (ACC-2)(SPCK, 1973) pp.70-73.

[13]   Buchanan, *ibid.*, p.7.

[14]   ACC, *Partners in Mission* (SPCK, 1973) pp.70-86.

Thereafter, there was little of pan-Anglican liturgical interest to be reported from either ACC meetings or the 1978 Lambeth Conference until 1985. ACC reports include a mention of a lectionary quest on one occasion (ACC-4, 1979), a *Filioque* concern on another (ACC-5, 1981), and a citing of liturgy as an identifying feature of Anglicanism on another (ACC-6, 1984). For ACC-6 in Nigeria Colin Buchanan had been asked to produce a report comparable to Ronald Jasper's in 1973; and as 'Liturgy 1973-84' it was (unlike Ronald Jasper's in 1973) arranged thematically rather than geographically. When the Secretary-General circulated it in advance, he added to it a report from the Primates' Meeting of October 1983, where a sub-group had tackled the question 'How does the Anglican Communion retain its traditional sense of unity?' This sub-group had also had attached to the question a second (somewhat leading) question about the place of the BCP in preserving unity. To this second question had been further added 'another paper, contributed from the Church of England, reinforcing an assumption that Anglican Unity was bound up in a clear way and to considerable extent with the Book of 1662'. So, nudged (and even provoked) in this way, the Primates' sub-group had attempted to answer the initial question in terms of liturgy, which led to their report being attached to Colin Buchanan's overview of a decade of liturgical change around the Anglican Communion. His overview was not reprinted in the published report of ACC-6, but references to liturgy in the actual report come in the context of this discussion of Anglican identity.[15] The published report also gave a page to initiation questions, and reprinted the relevant part of the Lambeth 1968 report and its resolution 25, reproduced on page 9 above.

Meanwhile all round the Communion revision of liturgies went ahead, in many cases with the prior rites of other provinces open in front of each. Booklets came and went; hardback books were authorized; parish editions appeared on the ground; and music, architecture, furnishings and ceremonial went into the melting-pot. Slowly, slowly, Africa, Asia and South America were joining in, seeking greater inculturation of the liturgy, yet seeking also for Anglican norms as part of their self-identification within the worldwide Communion.[16]

Could any viable form of co-ordination be brought to birth?

[15] Colin Buchanan's report, along with the Primates' sub-group's report, was published by him in Appendix 1 to his *Anglican Eucharistic Liturgy 1975-85* (Grove Liturgical Study 41, 1985) pp.24-32. This was a Study which he intended as an Introduction to his *Latest Anglican Liturgies 1976-1984* (Alcuin/SPCK, 1985) as this volume of eucharistic texts, unlike his two previous collections, had been stripped by the publishers of introductory material for reasons of economy, and Liturgical Study 41 thus filled the place of introductory material.

[16] The developments in official eucharistic liturgy from 1958 to 1985 are charted in Colin Buchanan's three collections of eucharistic liturgies. A later and wider survey of both liturgical themes and the revisions made in individual provinces is to be found in Charles Heffner and Cynthia Shattuck (eds), *The Oxford Guide to the Book of Common Prayer* (OUP, New York, 2006).

3. International Consultations Begin – IALC-1, Boston, 1985

From the 1960s onwards liturgical scholars from round the world and across the denominations began to meet each other every other year at the residential Congress of *Societas Liturgica*, the international ecumenical society of academic liturgists. During 1968-75 some of them also met on the International Consultation on English Texts (ICET), the organization which was seeking common English-language forms for classic elements in the liturgy, such as the Lord's Prayer and Sursum Corda.[17] When that task was accomplished, ICET ceased to meet from 1975. However, by the 1980s new issues had arisen in English usage (inclusive language being the most pressing), and members of several ecumenical liturgical bodies were asking whether it was not time to revisit the common ICET texts of a decade earlier. The North American Consultation on Common Texts (CCT) raised the question formally with its erstwhile partners from ICET - the Roman Catholic International Committee for English in the Liturgy (ICEL) and two ecumenical liturgical consultations: the British Joint Liturgical Group (JLG), and the Australian Consultation on Liturgy (ACOL). All agreed to hold a consultation to discuss this need of a new generation of common texts in English. The consultation duly occurred just before the 1983 *Societas* Congress in Vienna, and resulted in the formation of the English Language Liturgical Consultation (ELLC). This very use of the gathering of leading liturgists at *Societas* prompted David Holeton to raise with other Anglicans present the possibility of an international Anglican gathering also in conjunction with *Societas*. Those present encouraged him, and he went into partnership with Donald Gray from England to co-ordinate such a meeting when *Societas* met two years ahead in Boston. David Holeton, with an eye to the needs of the Communion as well as a strong personal academic interest, pressed as the central agenda item the admission of baptized children to communion prior to any age for confirmation. The two co-ordinators gave themselves wide discretion as to whom to invite and how to handle the programme – though inevitably Anglicans due to come to the *Societas* Congress, and thus enthusiasts already committed to the expense of travel, would provide a starting list of likely participants.

David Holeton had been in touch with the ACC since 1978 about lectionary issues, and, though lecturing in Vancouver, he was regularly in

---

[17] See page 10 above

London over the two years following 1983, often using the library at the Anglican Communion Office. In the process he very carefully and deliberately talked through the project with Canon Sam Van Culin, the Secretary-General of the ACC from 1982. Van Culin in turn encouraged the inauguration of the Consultation, and from his staff Deirdre Hoban supplied promising names from round the Communion – though the funding of travel from developing countries, as, eg, for David Gitari from Kenya, remained a virtually unassailable barrier. David Holeton secured accommodation in Boston for three days preceding the *Societas* Congress (i.e. for 29-31 July 1985), and set about inviting to the projected Consultation those Anglicans who had been at Vienna who would best relate to the projected theme, plus a very small number of others, and an 'ecumenical observer'. There finally gathered eight from Vienna[18], plus Eugene Fairweather from Toronto[19], Freddy Amoore from Southern Africa[20], Michael Vasey[21] from England, and Brian Davis[22], then Bishop of Waikato in New Zealand. Eugene Brand from the staff of the Lutheran World Fellowship, a scholar who had earlier written on the chosen topic, particpated as ecumenical observer. All met their own fares and paid their own way, unless they had persuaded home Liturgical Commissions or similar bodies to fund them. Preparatory papers were commissioned, a programme for the Consultation arranged, and a decision taken that Donald Gray should chair the meeting initially, with David Holeton as secretary. The 'Knaresborough' report from England, *Communion Before Confirmation?,* was distributed in duplicated form three months before being published and circulated to the General Synod in England. The two co-ordinators planned for a statement to be drafted and issued from the Consultation.

At the Consultation, despite a computer crash in which the first draft of a document was lost, the members of the Consultation were able to draft

[18] David Holeton (Canada), Donald Gray, Colin Buchanan, Kenneth Stevenson (England), Robert Brooks, Louis Weil, Leonel Mitchell (USA), and Ron Dowling (Australia). Kenneth Stevenson was valued not only for his scholarship, but also for the three different experiences he had had in his own life of being a child in the communion services of three different denominations, and particularly for his reflections on being included at the Table in one, and rejected in the others.

[19] Eugene Fairweather was a serious theologian, with a particular interest in children's participation in the eucharist, over which he had fought the Canadian House of Bishops for some years.

[20] Freddy Amoore was provincial secretary of the Church of the Province of South Africa and had been in correspondence over the matter in hand with David Holeton for some time, and was thus invited.

[21] Michael Vasey offered a balance through his evangelicalism (and proved invaluable in his computer skills, in the relatively early days of such technology). He was a member of GROW (see note 23 on page 14 overleaf and the outside back cover), which Colin Buchanan chaired, and, reading of the projected Consultation in *News of Liturgy* in early 1985, he asked to be invited, and, after momentary doubts, he was.

[22] Brian Davis, who had never seen himself as a liturgist, was induced to come because he had such widespread firsthand experience of ministering communion to children and of leading the way to changes in the provincial rules to enable this to happen.

and agree in two days a major set of findings, entitled 'The Boston Statement'. This treated water baptism as the sole sacramental initiation into Christ and his church, and urged that the proper concomitant of such initiation was the sharing in communion of all the baptized, without the imposition of other qualifications (or barriers), such as the rite of confirmation or the age of discretion. Grove Books Ltd agreed to publish the Statement itself immediately, and a collection of the papers in December.[23] Colin Buchanan edited this collection which was published as *Nurturing Children in Communion* (Grove Liturgical Study no. 44). The contents were not simply the preparatory papers, but were essays revised in the light of the actual Boston Consultation. Both the Statement and the Liturgical Study sold out within about five years, and the Statement and accompanying essays were then revisited in an American publication, Ruth Meyers (ed), *Children at the Table* (Church Hymnal Publication, New York, 1995). This included a new introductory essay by Colin Buchanan, a retouched form of most of the essays from *Nurturing Children in Communion*, and the Boston paper omitted in 1985 – Kenneth Stevenson on his sacramental experience as a child in three denominations.

The process of agreeing a Statement also required a defining of the gathering which had produced it. The members, acknowledging they were selectively invited and were all Western, affluent, white and male, made no claim to represent the whole Communion, but instead called themselves an 'International Anglican Liturgical Consultation'. They asked the two co-ordinators to convene a second such Consultation in tandem with the next Congress of *Societas*, scheduled for Brixen in the Dolomites in Northern Italy in August 1987.

The 'Recommendations' of the Boston Statement were:
'This Consultation recommends:
i)   that since baptism is the sacramental sign of full incorporation into the church, all baptized persons be admitted to communion.
ii)   that provincial baptismal rites be reviewed to the end that such texts explicitly affirm the communion of the newly baptized and that only one rite be authorized for the baptism whether of adults or infants so that no essential distinction be made between persons on basis of age.

---

[23] Colin Buchanan had owned the press until days beforehand, and was now the Company secretary, and, as chairman of the Group for Renewal Of Worship (GROW), which commissioned the Grove Liturgical Studies, could secure the publication timetable. He included the eight-page statement as the centrefold of the August edition of his monthly *News of Liturgy* (though it was also available separately).

iii) that in the celebration of baptism the vivid use of liturgical signs, e.g., the practice of immersion and the copious use of water be encouraged.

iv) that the celebration of baptism constitute a normal part of an episcopal visit.

v) that anyone admitted to communion in any part of the Anglican Communion be acknowledged as a communicant in every part of the Anglican Communion and not be denied communion on the basis of age or lack of confirmation.[24]

vi) that the Constitution and Canons of each Province be revised in accordance with the above recommendations; and that the Constitution and Canons be amended wherever they imply the necessity of confirmation for full church membership.

vii) that each Province clearly affirm that confirmation is not a rite of admission to communion, a principle affirmed by the bishops at Lambeth in 1968.[25]

viii) that the general communion of all the baptized assume a significant place in all ecumenical dialogues in which Anglicans are engaged.'

[24] [Original footnote in the Boston Statement] We note that one Province (Southern Africa) allows for the withdrawal of a child's communicant status in case of permanent removal to a parish other than where the child was admitted to communion. We also note that the Houses of Bishops in the United States and Canada have passed resolutions to ensure that a communicant anywhere in the Anglican Communion is a communicant everywhere within their respective churches.

[25] [Original footnote in the Boston Statement] Lambeth Conference 1968, *Resolutions and Reports* (London, 1968), p.37.

4. IALC-2, Brixen, 1987

Donald Gray and David Holeton, encouraged by the beginnings at Boston, duly planned a second Anglican Liturgical Consultation to come in 1987 at Brixen. In the process they burrowed away to gain official recognition – and possibly even some funding – from the ACC. Colin James, the Bishop of Winchester, chanced to be both chairman of the Church of England Liturgical Commission from early 1986 and also the Church of England episcopal representative on the ACC. He was, therefore, asked to carry the hopes of the convenors into the ACC meeting in Singapore in April 1987 (ACC-7). In fact he was not merely a messenger on behalf of IALCs, but had himself raised the question of a Anglican Communion Liturgical Commission as a separate enterprise prior to the meeting of the ACC. This concept proved attractive to the ACC, and is the key to what follows.

Consequently, ACC-7, while being polite and even encouraging about the concept of IALCs, found itself with other agenda for considering liturgy, and this threatened to complicate the worldwide scene which the IALC convenors were contemplating. In ACC-7's own order, there were three relevant agenda items as follows.

Firstly, they addressed the actual Boston agenda which, it will be recalled, were to be on the ACC agenda in any case as the outcome of the (slightly indistinct) resolutions passed at ACC-6 in 1984.[26] There were three pages of discussion (under 'Christian Initiation' rather than 'Liturgy'), their style somewhat defensive of the 'traditional' Anglican pattern. Following this came 'Resolution 10: Christian Initiation'. It did not refer to Boston, and hardly even indicated what the initiation issues were, but called for more education, sharing of information, and study at the next Lambeth Conference.

Secondly, their next item was 'D. Liturgical Matters'. This did refer to Boston and its sole half-page ran as follows:
> 'The preparatory papers for the Dogmatic and Pastoral section included the statement of an International Anglican Consultation held in Boston in July 1985 on Children and Communion, and a note from the Bishop of Winchester recommending that the second such Consultation planned for August in Northern Italy on Liturgical Education and Formation be "recognized" by the ACC, and that its successors be accorded some kind of official status.

---

[26] See page 11 above

Resolution 11: International Liturgical Consultations
THAT this Council:
(a) recognizes the 1987 Consultation, which is not to be funded by the ACC, and requests that its proceedings be made available to the ACC and the Lambeth Conference 1988;
(b) recommends that the membership of future consultations be widely representative of the Communion, and that the Secretary General be requested to confer with the organizers about its future meetings;
(c) encourages Provinces to give financial support for members of their Province who attend such gatherings.'

So far, this was probably all that could have been sought then from the ACC. However, the next (i.e. third) item was 'E. Proposal for an Anglican Communion Liturgical Commission.' Three full pages then expounded this proposal, with neither reference to 'Consultations', nor discussion of difficulties in the concept. The disproportionate weight given to it, compared with the treatment of IALC, indicated where the ACC's interests lay. The Council serenely adopted this proposal:

'Resolution 12: Anglican Communion Liturgical Commission
THAT this Council
Invites the Standing Committee to establish an Anglican Communion Liturgical Commission with the following terms of reference:
(a) to keep under review liturgical revision in the Anglican Communion, both among those Provinces which have gone a long way in this direction and those who have not;
(b) to offer encouragement, support and advice to those Provinces which have, as yet, few liturgically-trained specialists, whether in the pastoral or more theological aspects of liturgy, and in some instances finance the training of liturgists;
(c) to study and reflect on those areas in which inculturation and contextualization of Anglican worship is developing, maintaining contact with other Churches in those places as well as Anglican Provinces in other parts of the world;
(d) to study and evaluate ecumenical liturgical developments as they relate to the Anglican tradition;
(e) and, in doing all this, to attempt to discern liturgical features and principles in which, as the future unfolds, the Anglican Communion could recognize its continuing identity and encourage fellowship with other Christian Communions.

NB The cost of the Commission is estimated to be £8,000 per annum on the assumption that it will meet every two years and have a membership no less than the Inter-Anglican Theological and Doctrinal Commission (15 members).'

Well, the Brixen Consultation – IALC-2 – went ahead as planned. It was still unofficial, even if smiled upon by Sam Van Culin and greeted by a special message elicited from the Archbishop of Canterbury by Donald Gray. The theme was to be 'Liturgical Formation and Education', and David Holeton raised some money in Canada to enable liturgical scholars to attend from provinces where the costs of coming would have been beyond the scope of both official and unofficial funds. A notable new participant was Elisha Mbonigaba from Uganda, a student of David Holeton's in Vancouver, and he delivered a radical polemic against the Western cultural imperialism in relation to Anglican liturgy in Africa. A side-issue was handled in a paper by Colin Buchanan on 'The Bishop in Liturgy'. Donald Gray again assumed the chair, and the programme was duly carried through, and the papers were edited and published.[27] However, it was the constitutional position and role of IALCs present and future which overlaid other issues at the time; and to historians reflecting on it two decades later, these rank as far more significant than the theological content of the programme there.

Alarm had been created among the liturgists by the ACC Resolutions set out above. The IALC members, while welcoming Resolution 11, could not help but be disturbed by Resolution 12. Rumours on the breeze suggested that the ACC would never find the funding for a Liturgical Commission[28]; but there was no-one present at Brixen who had been at Singapore to interpret the mood of the members there or their grasp of the international liturgical situation.[29] So IALC-2 gave plenary time (with a small group drafting behind the scenes) to preparing a response, not only to confront the idea of a Commission, but also to chart the way for the future for Consultations. The upshot was the unanimously agreed 'Brixen Submission', as follows.

---

[27] The papers on the place of the laity were published as Tom Talley (ed), *The Liturgical Formation of the Laity: The Brixen Papers* (Alcuin/GROW Joint Liturgical Study no 5, Grove Books Ltd, 1988), and Colin Buchanan's paper led (at the request of the Consultation) to a symposium published with a view to the 1988 Lambeth Conference, Colin Buchanan (ed), *The Bishop in Liturgy: An Anglican Study* (Alcuin/GROW Joint Liturgical Study no 6, Grove Books Ltd, 1988). In the period since the Boston papers had been published as a 'Grove Liturgical Study', the Alcuin Club had approached GROW with a request that the existing series be turned into slightly larger 'Joint' Studies, under the aegis of a Joint Editorial Board, and with a spine. The Joint Board, chaired by Colin Buchanan, who, as recorded above, was also Grove Books company secretary, proved as open to IALC publications as GROW on its own had been in 1985.

[28] It is fundamental to the concept of an ACC Commission that ACC should fund it. Other unofficial or semi-official international Anglican agencies, such as networks or these 'Consultations', were to be distinguished from Commissions precisely in that there was no undertaking from ACC to fund them. ACC funds are notoriously scarce and new Commissions cannot be set in motion simply by votes or goodwill.

[29] Colin Craston later told Colin Buchanan that he had been cherishing a notion of such a commission since 1983.

THE 'BRIXEN SUBMISSION'

ANGLICAN LITURGICAL CONSULTATIONS

A submission by the Consultation held at Brixen, Italy, 23-26 August 1987, to the Standing Committee of the Anglican Consultative Council in response to the ACC proposal to form an International Anglican Liturgical Commission.

PREAMBLE

A   As the Archbishop of Canterbury said in his letter to the 1987 Consultation at Brixen 'Historically, the Anglican Church has found identity and coherence in its liturgy. Thus when questions are arising about our identity to-day there is urgent need for such a Consultation as yours. Liturgy both mirrors and shapes a Church, and Anglicans can learn much about each other through studying how our shared liturgical heritage is being applied and developed in different Provinces.'

B.   The Provinces and regional Churches of the Anglican Communion are self-governing. It is part of the spirit of Anglicanism to search for local expression of the historic Christian faith (cf Art. XXXIV), and to be committed to local ecumenism.

C.   The task of any Commission or Consultation would be to foster fellowship, scholarship, and understanding, and to respond when particular issues arise, but not to impose any programme on the Anglican Communion.

D.   The world of liturgical scholarship is increasingly ecumenical, which should be of great value to the Anglican Communion. Particularly this finds international expression in the biennial meetings of Societas Liturgica which draws together the major denominational traditions.

E.   The proposal that follows seeks to promote
(i)   access to developments in liturgical scholarship and practice
(ii)   proper representation of the Provinces
(iii)   the contribution of those with expertise in particular areas.
We recognize the need to balance continuity with open access, and wish to avoid the formation of a closed group.

PROPOSAL

A   That Consultations are a better method of proceeding for international Anglican purposes than would be a Standing Commission.

B   That ACC should nominate a steering group, with rotating membership of three or four people with recognized liturgical expertise, to convene, oversee, and guide such Consultations.

C   Biennial meetings in association with meetings of Societas Liturgica should be the normal occasions for such Anglican Liturgical Consultations (ALC), while not excluding the possibility of other meetings, should occasion arise.

D   That attendance should consist of
    (i)   those whom Provinces choose to nominate and send
    (ii)   Anglicans attending Societas Liturgica
    (iii) One or two others whom the steering group may invite.

E   That the business of the ALCs should be guided by the steering group, including in particular:
    (i)   matters referred by ACC
    (ii)   matters referred by particular Provinces.

F   That the procedures of ALCs should include the following:
    (i)   the steering group should write after each Consultation to notify Provinces of the next Consultation
    (ii)   in preparation for Consultations, if appropriate, the steering group should arrange for papers to be circulated in advance. It could also be helpful to prepare drafts of any statements in advance.
    (iii) that Consultations should normally proceed by consensus.
    (iv) accountability to ACC or its Standing Committee

G   That ACC funding be afforded in the first instance to enable the attendance of those nominated by Provinces unable to afford to fund participants themselves.

H   That ALCs would have no automatic authority over individual Provinces or their liturgical processes.

Donald Gray, England (Chairman)
David Holeton, Canada (Secretary)
Robert Brooks, USA
Evan Burge, Australia
Colin Buchanan, England
Daphne Fraser, England
Paul Gibson, Canada
Elisha Mbonigaba, Uganda

Robert McCullough, New Zealand
Richard Martin, USA
Harold Miller, Ireland
Bryan Spinks, England
Thomas Talley, USA
Gianfranco Tellini, Scotland
Michael Vasey, England
Themba Vundla, Southern Africa[30]

---

[30] All members of the Consultation signed this. Eugene Brand was again present as ecumenical observer, but, as a Lutheran and an observer, was not invited to sign the submission.

5. Getting Recognized – Lambeth 1988 and its Outcome

The Brixen Submission was duly forwarded to the ACC. It was followed up by actual meetings in the Winter months of 1987-88 between Donald Gray and David Holeton and Sam Van Culin, and further airing in frequent correspondence of the relative merits of the projected Commission and of the role of Consultations as envisaged at Brixen. This included the question as to whether Consultations with some restructuring could themselves fulfil the role envisaged for the Commission. No point of decision was reached, almost certainly because the 1988 Lambeth Conference was imminent, and the ACC Standing Committee was not due to meet until after it. As a general rule, it seemed policy issues could be postponed to see what emerged from the Lambeth Conference. Yet there was no attempt made in relation to this particular policy issue to brief the Conference or organize the agenda for the group that would work on liturgy. Neither the ACC-7 Resolution nor the IALC-2 Submission were mentioned in the half-baked liturgical material in the Blackheath preparatory document, which also ignored the ACC-7 recommendation that the Boston Statement should be made available to the Conference.

However, Colin Buchanan and Colin James were both members of the liturgy group in the Mission and Ministry Section of the Conference – and Brian Davis (by now Archbishop of New Zealand) was pressing the importance of the Boston Statement within the Section also. The Section Statement included in paragraph 194 (from the group considering liturgy) a neutral reference to the Boston Statement, alongside both an assertion that 'Baptism by water is the scriptural sacrament of once-for-all initiation into Christ...' (paragraph 192) and also a note that ACC-7 had raised questions over the Boston principles.[31] There was a footnote of attribution of the Boston Statement: 'This statement emerged from an international

---

[31] An unbalanced emphasis in the report upon the (somewhat prejudicial) questions raised by ACC-7 stemmed not from the group or section at Lambeth but from the editorial hand which during the following months determined the final text. Colin Buchanan, as secretary of the group, had to complain to the Secretary-General about this editorial alteration of the bishops' agreed text - see his *Lambeth and Liturgy 1988* (Grove Worship Series no. 106, 1989) pp.16-17. Brian Davis meanwhile provided his own personal resolution on the topic for the plenary Conference, and it was adopted as uncontroversial;
'69 ADMISSION TO COMMUNION
This Conference requests all Provinces to consider the theological and pastoral issues involved in the admission of those baptized but unconfirmed to communion (as set out in the Report of ACC-7), and to report their findings to the ACC.'

consultation of a number of Anglican liturgists, the first of a series of such consultations, which was held in Boston, Mass., USA 29-31 July 1985:' Perhaps the concept of IALCs (initially almost unknown to the members of that Lambeth group) was gently gaining currency. This group gave a 'steer' for future policy also in paragraph 180, addressing the ACC-7 call for a 'Commission':

> 'In this respect [i.e. regarding communication and co-ordination between provinces] we note the ACC-7 Resolution concerning the creation of an International Anglican Liturgical Commission. We request that the Standing Committee of the ACC, when it next meets, considers carefully how such a Commission could actually fulfil the hopes being placed upon it.'

The group also sponsored Resolution 47, which was adopted unanimously in plenary by the Conference:

> '47 LITURGICAL FREEDOM
> This Conference resolves that each Province should be free, subject to essential universal Anglican norms of worship, and to a valuing of traditional liturgical materials, to seek that expression of worship which is appropriate to its Christian people in their cultural context.'[32]

However, what nobody in the Mission and Ministry Section had anticipated was an onslaught from the Dogmatic and Pastoral Concerns Section. In paragraph 128 of their report (under the cross-heading 'Enhanced Role of the Primates') they put the mild hope:

> '...true doctrine...will involve special attention to the liturgies of the Churches. Encouragement, support and advice should be given to the Churches of the Communion in their work of liturgical revision. Mutual consultation regarding liturgical development and common reviews of the Prayer Books in use in the Communion should be envisaged. This should be a particular concern of the Primates...'

No-one reading the above would have visualized it was the launching pad (as it itself went on to claim) for the swingeing resolution 18.6 from that Section:

> 'This Conference...requests the Archbishop of Canterbury, with all the Primates of the Anglican Communion, to appoint an Advisory Body on Prayer Books of the Anglican Communion. The Body should be entrusted with the task of offering encouragement, support and advice to Churches of the Communion in their work of liturgical revision as well as facilitating mutual consultation

---

[32] Resolution 22, from a different Section, also included an urging to liturgical inculturation.

concerning, and review of, their Prayer Books as they are developed with a view to ensuring:

(a)   the public reading of the Scripture in a language understood by the people and instruction of the whole people of God in the scriptural faith by sermons and catechisms;

(b)   the use of the two sacraments ordained by Christ...

(c)   the use of forms of episcopal ordination to each of the three orders by prayer with the laying-on of hands;

(d)   the public recitation and teaching of the Apostles' and Nicene Creeds; and

(e)   the use of other liturgical expressions of unity in faith and life by which the whole people of God is nurtured and upheld, with continuing awareness of ecumenical liturgical developments.'

Colin Buchanan dubbed this the 'Policing Commission', as it was overtly a bid for a theological control of people who were viewed as untrustworthy – i.e. the writers of new liturgies. He moved an amendment to delete everything following 'Communion' in the second line and substitute 'to seek ways in which liturgical reform and renewal in the different provinces may be mutually communicated and, where possible, and subject to the needs of different cultural contexts, may also be co-ordinated.' This would have dispensed with the ' policing'. In his speech he asked whether the Conference really thought the liturgists were going to abandon the scriptures, sacraments, creeds and orders, and whether they needed a policing commission to keep them on the strait and narrow in these respects. Professor Stephen Sykes, a Theological Consultant working with the Dogmatic and Pastoral Concerns Section, responded vigorously, and both defeated the amendment and duly carried the original motion. Everyone in the know discerned that such an 'Advisory Body' could never be funded by the Communion, but a kind of quiet ideological struggle was going on underneath the practical proposal.

So much for the public front of the Conference. Behind it, and in the weeks following, negotiations were going on to bring some outcome from the Brixen Submission. The future of IALCs now faced threats of their being overborne by the ACC's proposed Liturgical Commission on the one hand, and by the Lambeth Conference's proposed Policing Commission on the other. Prompted by a letter from Colin Buchanan and Colin James about the former of these, an informal meeting was convened on 10 November for key persons available in London that day. Present were Colin Craston (chair of ACC), Sam Van Culin (secretary-general of ACC), Colin James (chairman of the Church of England Liturgical Commission, Church of England episcopal representative on ACC, and a member of the group on liturgy at the Lambeth Conference – and thus the obvious unofficial go-between), Donald Gray (one of the two convenors of the 1985 and 1987 IALCs), and Colin Buchanan (member of the 1985 and 1987 IALCs and secretary of the Lambeth group on liturgy). The agreed 'Notes' of this meeting include among 'Some agreements registered':

'When the ACC Standing Committee meets, it can tackle the tasks specified in the ACC Resolution in an item-by-item way. It *could* then resolve to act as follows:

A. To commend the planned 1989 Consultation and its subject of inculturation, and to seek ways in which it could be given more official endorsement (e.g. by the Primates), and also ways in which its published results could be commended to the Communion (e.g. by an Introduction by the Archbishop of Canterbury).

B. To ask the 1989 Consultation to report to the ACC on how a publication could set out ways in which common Anglican liturgical patterns could be conserved and promoted. Such a request *could* incorporate the unifying concerns which lie within the 'inculturation' Resolution 47 from the Lambeth Conference, and also the more explicit concerns of Resolution 18 and the 'Advisory Body'.

C. To suggest to the 1989 Consultation subject matter... for a prospective 1991 Consultation to consider.

D. Additionally, the Standing Committee would clearly be free, in terms of the ACC-7 Resolution, still to establish a Commission for the Communion...

E. Also additionally, the Standing Committee might wish to advise the Primates about how, in the light of the putative action set out above, the Lambeth Conference Resolution on an 'Advisory Body' might be implemented, or its proposed work absorbed by other means.'

It greatly helped the future of IALCs that both the 'Commission' desired by ACC-7 and the 'Advisory Body' desired by the Lambeth Conference were seen as somewhat remote (and costly) hypotheses over against the given fact of the very existence of IALCs. The issue of IALCs becoming a 'network' of the ACC was also raised, a pattern which would reflect that the expense of IALCs was met largely by their own members and by voluntary contributions, and this further helped give them credibility and standing in the eyes of the ACC persons. The outcome is represented by the minute and the resolution of the ACC Standing Committee from its meeting of 27 November to 3 December 1988:

Minutes of the Standing Committee of the ACC

(d) Informal Consultation on Liturgy

Canon Craston introduced notes of a meeting held between himself, Canon Van Culin, Canon Donald Gray, Bishop Colin James and Bishop Colin Buchanan in follow up to the resolutions of ACC-7 [Singapore 1987, proposing an international Liturgical Commission] on liturgy. Resolution 11 of ACC-7 had encouraged a group of liturgists due to meet at Brixen to submit their conclusions to the ACC and the Lambeth Conference. Resolution 12 of ACC-7 invited the Standing Committee to set up an Inter-Anglican Liturgical Commission. When the group met at Brixen the group wondered whether a full commission would in fact be doing work very much parallel to their own work. Accordingly, they had sent a submission to the ACC suggesting that instead of appointing a Liturgical Commission the ACC make use of their own programme and, if money were available, help send third world participants to their meetings. After some discussion the Standing Committee passed the following resolution:

Resolution 4

Resolved that -

The Standing Committee of the ACC, after receiving a report of the informal discussions between members of the international Anglican Liturgical Consultations and the Secretary-General, the Vice-Chairman of the ACC, and Bishop Colin James.-

(i)   welcomes the intention in the 1989 Consultation to explore further the subject of inculturation of worship within the common Anglican liturgical patterns we have inherited.

(ii)   invites the Consultation to submit its conclusions from the 1989 meeting to the Secretary General for circulation to the Primates' Meeting and the Standing Committee of the ACC for their consideration and possible commendation by the Primates to the Churches of the Communion.

(iii)   proposes that Bishop Colin James be convenor of the Consultation, if that is practicable at this stage, but in any case, be regarded as the Consultation's link with the Primates' Meeting.

(iv)   strongly recommends the invitation of representatives of Churches not at present in the Consultation group, funding being from Churches already represented in the group, the ACC Standing Committee being ready to suggest names.

(v)   recommends that in the light of financial difficulties a Liturgical Commission should not be appointed, while recognizing the part a Commission might play in helping the Communion to express its continuing identity, self-understanding and vocation within the one, holy Catholic and Apostolic Church.

There was much encouragement for the IALCs from this; and the idea of a Liturgical Commission for the Communion never surfaced again. The Policing Commission was not technically ACC's business, as Lambeth Resolution 18 was directed to the Primates. However, when the Primates met in May 1989, they took no steps to implement it – though it was not forgotten. They did approve the role for Colin James proposed by the ACC Standing Committee, as shown above, though in the terms of paragraph (iii) he became the 'link' rather than the convenor. They also accepted an offer by Michael Peers, the Primate of the Anglican Church in Canada, to second that Church's Liturgical Officer, Paul Gibson, to work part-time for the ACC as its 'Co-ordinator for Liturgy'. Paul Gibson had been present in his Canadian capacity at Brixen, and was now to play an increasing role in the administration of IALCs. He also thereafter regularly attended meetings of the ACC itself, and not only contributed professionally to the agenda, but also provided a further link with IALCs.

Colin James, thus approved by the ACC, duly booked himself in for IALC-3, being convened by Donald Gray and David Holeton at York that Summer, and the scene was set for a constitution to be adopted and a medium-term stability to be given to the wobbly but lively young organization.

6. IALC-3, York, 1989

Boston had 12 members, Brixen 16, but 31 were booked in for York. Rather like Brixen it was to have a double thrust – both theological agenda and a constitutional advance.

Partly arising from Elisha Mbonigaba's polemic at Brixen and partly from the theme of the *Societas* Congress at York which was also liturgical inculturation, the co-ordinators had decided on inculturation of the liturgy as the topic for IALC. Contributors from round the world were invited, and their presentations widened horizons and opened new questions. For the first time there were participants from Ghana, Nigeria, and Sri Lanka, joining with another Ugandan and the more established 'Western' members. In a few cases funding had been provided from these latter for the newcomers to attend; and the Consultation gave itself to agreeing a major Statement, which it entitled 'Down to Earth Worship: Liturgical Inculturation and the Anglican Communion'. It took its cue from the two Lambeth Conference Resolutions (nos 22 and 47) on inculturation, and began by quoting them both.[33] The statement then outlined principles and added illustrative examples to give force to the direction of the resolutions. It remains to the present time a major signpost for Anglican liturgical development. The Consultation also adopted two minor statements: the first expressing concern about over-rigid copyright protection of liturgical texts, and the second supporting the concept of a fixed Easter.

However, in the light of history, the adoption of a constitution and official affiliation to the ACC has been of equal or greater significance. The document's title was 'The Structure of Anglican Liturgical Consultations: Anglican Liturgical Consultations Guidelines', and it has been known ever since as the 'Guidelines'. Its preamble expressed gratitude for the secondment of Paul Gibson to become Co-ordinator for Liturgy to the ACC, and maximized the significance of links between the Consultations and the ACC. The section on principles laid weight upon developments in liturgical scholarship and practice and the need for communication and cross-fertilization across the whole spectrum of Anglican provinces (including the financial implications of finding participants from ill-funded provinces). The final section set out qualifications for membership, and the provision of an elected Steering Committee to ensure that Consultations

---

[33] Resolution 47, devised by the Lambeth group on liturgy, is quoted on page 23 above; and Resolution 22 (which came from a different group) was similar.

were duly planned and executed.[34] This Committee was to include 'one member of ACC appointed by the Standing Committee of ACC to be a link with ACC and the Primates meeting.' The Guidelines have been marginally amended at later Consultations, but have endured as the constitutional basis of the Consultations.

IALC-3, thus constituted by its own decision in plenary, then elected a Steering Committee of David Holeton from Canada, Themba Vundla from Southern Africa, and Rod McCullough from Aotearoa, New Zealand; Colin James continued as the link with the ACC. Under the provisions, the candidate with the highest number of votes at the election would serve until the second Consultation from the point of election, while the others would serve simply until the next one. In this first election it was David Holeton who was thus accorded a two-term stint, and the Steering Committee unsurprisingly elected him as their chair. He was thus established as the first constituted chair of IALCs (in contrast with the previous informal arrangement of two persons convening, with one of them then acting as chair during the actual meetings). However, for lack of finance for worldwide travel, this first Steering Committee could only actually meet at the conclusion of the York Consultation, and again a day or so before the beginning of the next one – IALC-4 in Toronto.[35]

The Guidelines were published along with the text of 'Down to Earth Worship' and the two minor statements in pamphlet form, David Holeton (ed), *Findings of the Third International Anglican Liturgical Consultation* (Grove Books Ltd, 1989). The theological and practical papers from York were also edited by David Holeton and were published with the 'Down to Earth Worship' Statement as *Liturgical Inculturation in the Anglican Communion* (Alcuin/GROW Joint Liturgical Study no.15, Grove Books Ltd, 1990). These were published in June 1990 in time for ACC-8, which was meeting in Wales in July. ACC-8 then published both 'Down to Earth Worship' and the Guidelines in its official report.[36] Its resolutions included a welcoming of the appointment of Paul Gibson as Co-ordinator for

---

[34] This steering agency had been called the 'Steering Group' in the Brixen Submission, and has often been so called since. But the Guidelines and other documents have called it the 'Steering Committee', and that nomenclature is adopted throughout in this Study.

[35] During the two-year period Rod McCullough resigned from the Steering Committee for personal reasons and Ron Dowling (Australia) was invited to fill his place partly to retain the geographical balance.

[36] ACC, *Mission in a Broken World: Report of ACC-8 Wales 1990* (CHP, 1990) pp.172-180. Very oddly, the footnote in 'Down to Earth Worship' which mentions (and gently sets aside) the infamous resolution 18.6 of Lambeth 1988 quoted on pages 23-24 above, appears on page 177 as though it were the conclusion of the Statement, partly because it is in the same typesize as the Statement itself, though very close examination reveals that it is fact running on from the footnote on the facing page.

Liturgy, and a handing on to him of responsibility for calendar issues raised by resolution 60 of Lambeth 1988, and for gathering reports from member churches as to their response to resolution 69 about admission to communion.[37] There was also a resolution with direct reference to IALCs:

'Resolution 10: Third International Anglican Liturgical Consultation

This Council:

(a) receives with appreciation the statement "Down to Earth Worship" (Appendix 1 on p.172 below), commends it and the companion essays *of Liturgical Inculturation in the Anglican Communion* to the member Churches for study, invites them to send their responses and further exampls of liturgical inculturation to the Co-ordinator for Liturgy, and expresses appreciation to the members of the International Anglican Liturgical Consultation for their thoughtful and helpful work on behalf of the Communion;

(b) welcomes the Guidelines (Appendix II, p.177) set out in the findings of the third International Anglican Liturgical Consultation, and believes that the Consultations have a continuing and important role in addressing liturgical issues affecting the Anglican Communion.'

IALCs had arrived.

---

[37] Resolution 69 is reprinted in footnote 31 on page 22 above.

7. IALC-4, Toronto, 1991

IALC-4 was, following custom and the Guidelines, to come in tandem with the Congress of *Societas* in Toronto in August 1991. Its theme, determined by the Steering Committee before they left York, was to be Christian Initiation, an opportunity to take the Boston findings further. While, as shown above, the Steering Committee could not meet again before the Toronto Consultation itself, David Holeton was then located near to Paul Gibson in Toronto, and was also regularly in England for family reasons, and was thus able to liase with Colin James. The charter was now clear, to invite participants from every province. Both the goodwill of the Anglican Church in Canada and the personal influence of Colin James provided some bursary funds; and these enabled the Steering Committee also to offer help for those invited from provinces unable to fund participants themselves. The upshot was an attendance double that at York - actually 63 plus Eugene Brand, now dubbed 'ecumenical partner', and they were drawn from 19 churches or provinces and also from the extra-provincial dioceses of Cuba and Sri Lanka. David Holeton later characterized the Consultation as 'a representative body which includes most of the liturgical scholars active in the Anglican Communion'.[38] Serious preparation was provided by weighty resource papers in advance, and the Consultation tackled the theme under four heads: the renewal of initiation theology; baptism, mission and ministry; confirmation and the renewal of baptismal faith; rites of initiation.[39] At the end there emerged from the four sections an 8,000-word Toronto Statement, 'Walk in Newness of Life', which was then adopted, almost by consensus, by the Consultation as a whole.[40] It built upon the Boston recommendations[41], and incorporated them into its text, and provided its own as follows:

---

[38]   David Holeton (ed.), *Growing in Newness of Life: Christian Initiation in Anglicanism Today* (ABC, Toronto, 1993) p.13.

[39]   In addition, the Consultation had been asked by the Standing Committee of the ACC to prepare a paper on 'Liturgy and Evangelism'. In fact the agenda did not permit time to be given to this, and it was held over. See page 37 below.

[40]   Two Englishmen, a Welshman and a West African voted against Recommendation (c), and one Englishman abstained and one voted against in respect of incorporating the Boston Recommendations.

[41]   See the text of these on pages 14-15 above.

RECOMMENDATIONS
of the
Fourth International Anglican Liturgical Consultation
at Toronto 1991 on
PRINCIPLES OF CHRISTIAN INITIATION

a. The renewal of baptismal practice is an integral part of mission and evangelism. Liturgical texts must point beyond the life of the church to God's mission in the world.
b. Baptism is for people of all ages, both adults and infants. Baptism is administered after preparation and instruction of candidates, or where they are unable to answer for themselves, of their parent(s) or guardian(s).
c. Baptism is complete sacramental initiation and leads to participation in the eucharist. Confirmation and other rites of affirmation have a continuing pastoral role in the renewal of faith among the baptized but are in no way to be seen as a completion of baptism or as necessary for admission to communion.
d. The catechumenate is a model for preparation and formation for baptism. We recognize that its constituent liturgical rites may vary in different cultural contexts.
e. Whatever language is used in the rest of the baptismal rite, both the profession of faith and the baptismal formula should continue to name God as Father, Son, and Holy Spirit.
f. Baptism once received is unrepeatable and any rites of renewal must avoid being misconstrued as rebaptism.
g. The pastoral rite of confirmation may be delegated by the bishop to a presbyter.

Other business was done, including reports from different provinces, and a presentation by Paul Gibson of work he was doing on the recognition of saints and heroes within the Communion. However, Toronto inevitably went down in history for its Statement. Steps were taken quickly to publish this as a Grove Booklet, David Holeton (ed), *Christian Initiation in the Anglican Communion* (Grove Worship Series no.118, 1991); and in due course the resource papers, updated to take the actual Statement into account and accompanied by new material commissioned to promote the implementation of its principles, were published with the Statement itself in a weighty symposium, David Holeton (ed), *Growing in Newness of Life: Christian Initiation in Anglicanism Today* (ABC, Toronto, 1993).

A happy feature of the membership of the Consultation was that Brian Davis reappeared, and, as he was now Primate of New Zealand as well as the New Zealand episcopal representative on the ACC, it was hoped he would in due course take over from Colin James as the link with the Primates' meeting and the ACC. For the Steering Committee David Holeton was still in place, while the charter of the other two expired at Toronto. Three more members were now elected to join David Holeton: Ron Dowling (Australia)(who gained the most votes), David Gitari (Kenya) and Ruth Meyers (USA). David Holeton was confirmed as chair by the Committee. Paul Gibson was now available to service the meetings of the Committee, and, through the provident inclusion of a fee towards IALC funds within the charge for participating at Toronto, finances were available from then on to enable the Steering Committee physically to meet between Consultations. On the other hand, Colin James had warned that it was not politic to go back to grant-making persons and agencies every two years, and he advised a four-year interval before the next full Consultation. This was confirmed by Paul Gibson in relation to his finding grants within the Anglican Church of Canada. The Steering Committee took the point, and, as, following the mind of those at Toronto, they scheduled the theme for the next Consultation to be the eucharist, they also started to think in terms of that full Consultation being in Dublin in 1995, and of an 'interim' meeting being held in tandem with the *Societas* Congress due at Friburg in Switzerland in 1993. The interim 'conference' would not have funds for bursaries, would not make Statements, and would not have new elections, as the Steering Committee was appointed to run until the next full Consultation. On the other hand, with a topic as vast and demanding as the eucharist, an interim conference, convened under the auspices of the Steering Committee, could do valuable work in preparation for a full Consultation.

8. 1991-1995 – An Intermediate Period

Toronto had undoubtedly seen IALCs come of age. The Consultation itself had been a success, both in numbers and in the quality of its work, and its far-reaching Statement was quickly in print. Its constitution was in full operation, and the Steering Committee, with funds available and Paul Gibson to service it, could address its task confidently. However, the projected four-year gap until the next Consultation presented problems, not least a sense of discontinuity from one Consultation to the next, and a reduced expectation that persons nominated for one Consultation would reappear in strength at the next. The immediate task, however, when the Steering Committee met at Colin James' invitation at Winchester in July 1992 and accepted Colin James' advice about funding, was to plan the preparatory, or 'interim', conference in August 1993, a gathering to which only those who could pay their own way would be able to come.

Cape Town January 1993

In ways that might not have been foreseen two years before, two other events of significance then intervened in the first half of 1993. The first of these came at the joint meeting of the ACC and the Primates in Cape Town in January of that year. Paul Gibson gave the joint meeting a weighty account of his own activities, but went further in making recommendations from the responsibilities given to him at ACC-8 in 1990 thus bringing his own expertise to the meeting. His impact included a commendation of the Revised Common Lectionary, an urging that the Provinces should study the Toronto Statement, a very full document of his own on principles of Calendar Revision, including the issue of recognition and commemoration of saints and heroes of the Christian faith, and a delightful deflection of the 1988 Lambeth Resolution 18 about a 'policing commission', a deflection which is best understood through the words of the actual Cape Town Resolution:

> 'Resolution 16 – Advisory Body on Prayer Books
> Resolved, that this Joint Meeting of the Primates of the Anglican Communion and the Anglican Consultative Council, in reference to Resolution 18 of the Lambeth Conference 1988 (requesting the appointment of an Advisory Body on Prayer Books of the Anglican Communion),
>> endorses the general recommendation made in the Report of the Co-Ordinator for Liturgy and in particular the recommendation that the various Conferences, Councils, and

> Provinces of the Anglican Communuion recognize and use
> these Consultations [viz, the IALCs[42]] as the appropriate
> channels through which liturgical issues can be discussed and
> liturgical norms discerned; and

> Requests the Co-Ordinator for Liturgy to facilitate work in
> this area.'

The Cape Town meeting thus achieved two major results, though possibly
without sufficient memory of the 1988 Lambeth debate on Resolution 18
to understand the full significance of those results. Firstly, the participants
finally removed the 'policing' sting from the policy stated in the Lambeth
Resolution; and, secondly, they accorded to the liturgists themselves
(whom the movers at Lambeth had wanted to be subject to policing) the
proactive role of advice and encouragement towards the various provincial
liturgical committees. There was from then on no possibility of any other
Commission or 'Advisory Body' being constituted to fulfil an official
Anglican Communion role in liturgy. At this meeting also it was agreed
that Brian Davis would indeed succeed Colin James as the link person with
the Primates and ACC.

The second significant event of the first half of 1993 was the Kanamai
Consultation on inculturation of the liturgy in Africa. This was held at
Kanamai, near Mombasa on the Kenyan coast, from 31 May to 4 June
1993, under the auspices of CAPA, the Council of Anglican Provinces in
Africa. It was initiated by David Gitari, then Bishop of Kirinyaga in Kenya,
who had first got together the African participants at Toronto and urged a
pan-African conference upon them. He then not only got the backing of
CAPA but also touched major British missionary societies for financial
assistance, and took on responsibility for organizing and convening the
Consultation. Members came from ten of the 12 African provinces, with a
total of 17 such participants, and they were assisted by 20 Kenyan
Anglicans hosting them and six guest consultants from elsewhere in the
Anglican Communion. David Gitari emphasized at the Consultation the
responsibility that those who had been at Toronto now had to disseminate
the Toronto Statement in Africa, a policy which ran counter to deeply
entrenched practice in most parts of the continent in relation to the role
of confirmation as affording admission to communion. For its own
agenda, the Consultation worked in groups and finally adopted a resultant
Statement, 'African Culture and Anglican Liturgy'. This was weighty in its
content and wide in its scope, and in principle went a long way to meet

---

[42]   [Editorial footnote] Slightly comically, there is no grammatical antecedent to 'these Consultations'
     anywhere in the Cape Town report, but the reference to Paul Gibson's recommendations makes the
     meaning sure.

the African concerns expressed by Elisha Mbonigaba at Brixen (which he had pressed again at Kanamai) and adopted by the whole Consultation at York. The statement was published in the first instance as a pamphlet included in the July 1993 edition of *News of Liturgy*, but also available separately. A little later the presentations were published in larger form with the statement and with a response from the Nigerian, Solomon Amusan, who had been unable to get to Kanamai. These were brought together in David Gitari (ed), *Anglican Liturgical Inculturation in Africa: The Kanamai Statement 'African Culture and Anglican Liturgy'* (Alcuin/GROW Joint Liturgical Study no.28, Grove Books, 1994). The CAPA Consultation ended with the appointment of a continuation committee and a mandate to convene another Consultation three years from then.

Untermachtal August 1993
Then on 9-13 August came the Untermachtal Conference, beginning work on the eucharist. 38 persons attended as members (with Anita Stauffer from the Lutheran World Federation, resident in Switzerland, as ecumenical partner). These were almost entirely from 'first world' countries, for the financial reasons already set out above, and the only exception was Juan Quevedo-Bosch from Cuba. The process followed was to have two main papers, and for the rest of the time have the members work in groups to identify issues under a great series of different headings. The conference has become famous in memory for the paper delivered by Tom Talley on 'Eucharistic Prayers, Past, Present and Future'. With typical combination of depth of scholarship with thrust of advocacy he drew from both history and contemporary examples principles of the structure to be sought in a eucharistic prayer. In the process he commended a broadly 'Eastern' pattern of narrative, anamnesis and epiclesis, and located it in a larger framework of the whole prayer by characterizing such a pattern as the 'Trinitarian structure'. The other main paper was written by one of the two present authors and edited by the other into an intelligible shape and dealt with precedents for change in Anglican eucharists, with particular reference to the 20th century. The groups produced short treatments opening up the issues under 15 headings. The papers were collected and published as David R. Holeton (ed*), Revising the Eucharist: Groundwork for the Anglican Communion – Studies in Preparation for the Dublin Consultation* (Alcuin/GROW Joint Liturgical Studies no. 27, Grove Books, 1994). It is to this volume that students must go for the Talley essay.

The conference also handled two other concerns. One was to receive a report commissioned from Canadian member Matthew Johnson on the question of the transmission of disease by the common cup. At a time when AIDS was a growing concern around the world, there was fear in some quarters that it could be transmitted by the chalice and, in some parts of the Communion, there were moves towards intinction rather than drinking from the common cup. The report, written in conjunction with two immunologists, concluded that AIDS could not be contracted by sharing the common cup, thus preserving a fundamental symbol of eucharistic eating and drinking. The other picked up the request from the ACC Standing Committee for a statement on 'Liturgy and Evangelism'.[43] Some advance papers had been prepared and the whole conference spent time in groups discussing these, before remitting a drafting task to a small group. This group in turn produced a paper which the conference adopted as its response to the original request, and passed to the Steering Committee to edit it and submit it.

The Steering Committee then met at the end of the Untermachtal conference and, with Brian Davis now present, met again in Berkeley, California, in June 1994. They had already booked the premises for the full Consultation in Dublin in 1995, while working hard at fund-raising and alerting the Provinces as to the availability of bursaries for participants at Dublin. Money came from various sources, including some Anglican synodical bodies or individual bishops and a parish foundation approached by Ruth Meyers in the USA. Colin Buchanan trailed a coat successfully in *News of Liturgy* specifically to raise funds from its readers to bring one such bursar, Solomon Amusan, from Nigeria.

---

[43] This had originally gone to IALC-4 at Toronto (see note 39 on page 31 above), but had been held over there by the Steering Committee.

9. IALC-5, Dublin, 1995

So it was that 71 persons from 19 Provinces (plus a new ecumenical partner, the Jesuit liturgist, John Baldovin) met at the Church of Ireland College of Education in Rathmines (Dublin) from 8 to 12 August 1995. Eight African provinces had been enabled to send a participant, and in six cases those participants had also been at Kanamai. The Steering Committee had divided the subject matter under five headings: (i) eucharistic theology; (ii) ministry, order and the eucharist; (iii) the structure of the eucharist; (iv) eucharist: ritual, language and symbolism; (v) liturgical and eucharistic renewal. The Consultation then worked in five groups on these themes, and between them produced five separate statements running to around 16,000 words in all. Under the constraints of time it would not have been possible to get these separate statements adopted in plenary as the findings of the whole Consultation. Instead they were conserved as section reports within the major document from the whole Consultation, and the plenary session adopted unanimously 'Principles and Recommendations'. These were:

1   In the celebration of the eucharist, all the baptized are called to participate in the great sign of our common identity as the people of God, the body of Christ, and the community of the Holy Spirit. No baptized person should be excluded from participating in the eucharistic assembly on such grounds as age, race, gender, economic circumstance or mental capacity.

2   In the future, Anglican unity will find its liturgical expression not so much in uniform texts as in a common approach to eucharistic celebration and a structure which will ensure a balance of word, prayer and sacrament, and which bears witness to the catholic calling of the Anglican Communion.

3   The eucharistic action models the way in which God as redeemer comes into the world in the Word made flesh, to which the people of God respond by offering themselves – broken individuals – to be made one body in Christ's risen life. This continual process of transformation is enacted in each celebration.

4   The sacrificial character of all Christian life and worship must be articulated in a way that does not blur the unique atoning work of Christ. Vivid language, symbol, and metaphor engage human memory and assist the eucharistic action in forming the life of the community.

5   In the eucharist, we encounter the mystery of the triune God in the proclamation of the word and the celebration of the sacrament. The

fundamental character of the eucharistic prayer is thanksgiving and the whole eucharistic prayer should be seen as consecratory. The elements of memorial and invocation are caught up within the movement of thanksgiving.

6   In, through, and with Christ, the assembly is the celebrant of the eucharist. Among other tasks it is appropriate for lay persons to play their part in proclaiming the word, leading the prayers of the people, and distributing communion. The liturgical functions of the ordained arise out of pastoral responsibility. Separating liturgical function and pastoral oversight tends to reduce liturgical presidency to an isolated ritual function.

7   The embodied character of Christian worship must be honoured in proclamation, music, symbol, and ritual. If inculturation is to be taken seriously, local culture and custom which are not in conflict with the Gospel must be reflected in the liturgy, interacting with the accumulated inculturation of the tradition.

8   The church needs leaders who are themselves open to renewal and are able to facilitate and enable it in community. This should affect the liturgical formation of laity and clergy, especially bishops as leaders of the local community. Such continuing formation is a priority and adequate resources for it should be provided in every Province.

9   Celebrating the eucharist involves reaffirming the baptismal commitment to die to self and be raised to newness of life, and embodying that vision of the kingdom in searching for justice, reconciliation and peace in the community. The Spirit who calls us into one body in Christ equips and sends us out to live this divine life.

The Dublin Statement was duly published as David Holeton (ed), *Renewing the Anglican Eucharist* (Grove Worship Series 135, 1996); and in due course, as with Toronto, this was followed by a volume of essays, David Holeton (ed), *Our Thanks and Praise* (Anglican Book Centre, Toronto, 1998).

At the end of the Dublin Consultation, Ron Dowling (Australia) was due to continue on the Steering Committee until the next Consultation. The terms of the other three members expired, and the election provided Sister Jean Campbell OSH (USA)(with the highest vote), Solomon Amusan (Nigeria), and Colin Buchanan (England). The new Steering Committee asked Ron Dowling to take the chair, and reckoned their next topic would be ministry and ordination, and that, with this topic, an interim conference should be planned for August 1997 in Finland, and the next full Consultation would be in Kottayam in South India in 1999.

10. From Dublin to Lambeth 1995-1998

Ron Dowling led the new Steering Committee, and was immediately invited by the new Secretary-General of the ACC, John Peterson, to a gathering in London in December 1995 of the convenors of all the ACC's recognized 'networks'.[44] Paul Gibson also participated, and they learned that, among the networks, IALC was ahead of the field for communication, meetings, and actual output. This venture has not been repeated since – no doubt for lack of finance.

In 1996 ACC-10 met in October in Panama. Its report contains not only a personal report by Paul Gibson, and a complete reprinting of the Dublin statement, but also the report of a Section which was considering in depth 'Looking to the Future in Worship'.[45] While Paul Gibson participated in this Section's work, the members included none known as liturgists (though Brian Davis was there, and Dinis Sengulane of Lebombo had been in the group on liturgy at the 1988 Lambeth Conference), and the report showed no connection with IALCs or their Statements – possibly just because Paul Gibson's report was appearing elsewhere in the volume.

The Steering Committee's own next meeting after Dublin was held in Johannesburg on 14-17 November 1996.[46] This was Brian Davis' last participation as the link person with the Primates, for he contracted cancer soon after, resigned his archiepiscopate, and died during 1997. *Societas Liturgica* was to meet in Turku, Finland, in 1997, so a Finnish venue was sought for an 'interim' conference on ordination. In the same way as the Untermachtal gathering had done with the eucharist, this would prepare for a full Consultation on ordination in 1999 (when *Societas* would be meeting in Kottayam, South India). Paul Bradshaw and David Holeton surveyed the ground in Finland in November 1995 on behalf of *Societas*, while at the same time looking out for a venue for this IALC 'conference'.

---

[44] 'Networks' is an umbrella title for all ACC recognizeed bodies or agencies which are not 'Commissions'. The distinguishing point is that commissions are funded by the ACC (see the references to projected commissions in note 28 on page 18 and references on page 24).

[45] ACC, *Being Anglican in the Third Millennium* (Morehouse, Harrisburg, 1997) pp.113-117, 281-339, and 143-150 respectively.

[46] The Steering Committee enjoyed an invitation to meet in Johannesburg in November 1996 in tandem with the second CAPA Consultation on liturgy, which they were thus enabled to attend as guests. It has to be said that this second CAPA Consultation, in the absence of David Gitari (who was at his own House of Bishops, being elected Archbishop of Kenya that week), contrasted sadly with the first one at Kanamai, Kenya, in June 1993 (see pages 35-36 above). The guest speakers were not briefed, and the participants were neither given a sense of direction nor enabled to reach any conclusion.

In the event, while *Societas'* numbers decreed its Congress should go to Turku, space enough for IALC was found at Järvenpää, a conference centre near to Helsinki, for five days prior to the Congress of *Societas*.[47] The topic of ministry and ordination, taken in sequence with the two previous Consultations on initiation and eucharist, was now beginning to mirror the sequence of the 1982 Lima ecumenical document, *Baptism – Eucharist – Ministry*, and this at intervals thereafter became explicit.

Järvenpää 1997

Preparatory papers were circulated and 46 persons met at Järvenpää from 4 to 9 August 1997. When the conference convened, a new representative of the Primates, Archbishop Ellison Pogo of Melanesia, had joined the Steering Committee in place of Brian Davis. Certain problems were encountered in addressing the subject – partly that the varied practice of ministry (along with issues of vocation, selection and training) was pulling minds away from liturgical texts and practice, and partly that many persons experienced in the worship of their own provinces nevertheless were rarely if ever present at ordinations, which were correspondingly unfamiliar to them. A cross-current was also blowing as to whether a 'permanent diaconate' had mileage on the one hand, and whether 'direct ordination' (eg of a lay person being ordained direct to the presbyterate without first being ordained deacon) should be commended and adopted on the other. A series of papers was collected and published, David R.Holeton (ed), *Anglican Orders and Ordinations* (Alcuin/GROW Joint Liturgical Study 39, Grove Books, Cambridge, 1998).

Before the full Consultation could then occur in Kottayam, as the Steering Committee were planning, the 1998 Lambeth Conference intervened. For the first time in the history of the Conferences, provinces were actively encouraged to make 'their' worship event at the Conference (in three weeks they took on one event each) truly and culturally their own. However, the group in Section 3 (on 'Ministry and Mission') which had responsibility for preparing a Statement on liturgy had its work summarily obliterated by the opposition to it of Section 4 on 'Called to be One' led by Stephen Sykes, Bishop of Ely. The whole Lambeth Statement was consequently silent on the issue of liturgy.[48] However, the group, chaired in the second week by Colin Buchanan, was able to draft one plenary

---

[47] Järvenpää was the place where the 'Porvoo' Declaration was agreed in 1992, but the Declaration was named 'Porvoo' (the location of the cathedral to which, on completion of the task, the participants adjourned for a service of thanksgiving) on the grounds that 'Järvenpää' was unlikely to be memorable or even sayable for the future.

[48] This sorry episode is written up by Colin Buchanan in his *Taking the Long View* (CHP, London, 2006), and the draft statement that was blocked was published by him unofficially in NOL in September 1998, and is reproduced here as the appendix on pages 54-56 below.

resolution in support of IALC, along with two others about liturgy, all three of which came from that Section. Section 4, which had torpedoed the draft statement, then also presented a petition to say that this pro-IALC resolution was controversial. This meant that, instead of going through 'on the nod', the resolution would be debated – and, if 'controversial' meant anything, it would be opposed by those who had signed the petition. However, in plenary, when the resolution was called, the opposition had melted away and no voices contrary to widespread confidence in IALCs were heard. Instead the resolution was marginally amended in an anodyne way by Kenneth Stevenson (England) with the support of George Connor (Aotearoa), both of them bishops who had participated in IALCs. The resolution then went through *nem.con.* as the third of these three relevant resolutions:

'Resolution III.14

Inculturation of Worship

This Conference, rejoicing in its own experience of multi-cultural worship, reaffirms Resolutions 22 and 47 of the 1988 Lambeth Conference encouraging the inculturation of worship and urges each province to seek the best ways of inculturating its forms and practice of worship.

Resolution III.15

Co-ordinator for Liturgy

This Conference:
(a) thanks the Anglican Church of Canada for seconding the Revd Paul Gibson to the Anglican Consultative Council (ACC) in 1989 and for funding his work, and is grateful for his contribution to the Anglican Communion as its Co-ordinator for Liturgy in the years since then.
(b) urgently requests the Anglican Consultative Council to take steps to find, appoint and sustain a successor to him on his retirement; and
(c) calls upon all provinces to keep the Anglican Consultative Council fully informed about all official liturgical revision through the Co-ordinator for Liturgy or other members of the Council's staff as necessary.

Resolution III.16

International Anglican Liturgical Consultations

This Conference welcomes the emergence in the 1980s of the International Anglican Liturgical Consultations (IALCs); endorses the recognition given to the IALCs by, first the Standing Committee of the Anglican Consultative Council (ACC) and then in 1993, by the Joint Meeting of the Primates and the ACC; requests the IALCs to report regularly to the Primates' Meeting; commends to study of each diocese and province the publications of the IALCs; asks each province to send representatives to the Consultations held every four years in order that these may represent the whole Communion; and commends to the provinces which can afford to send more representatives the principle of funding bursaries for those provinces which cannot.'

The overall outcome of these resolutions is not wholly coherent or clearcut. III.15 looks as though the 1993 decision to which III.16 refers had been entirely ignored. However, what it highlighted about Paul Gibson's own role was valuable; and when Paul Gibson reached official retirement a year later, he was retained by the ACC in an honorary capacity, in which the Council still funded his travel for IALC purposes, and provided a modest honorarium . Thus the IALC Steering Committee itself could also gratefully retain him to provide secretarial and administrative back-up for their work. Resolution III.16, despite the hostile labelling of it as 'controversial', put down useful markers. Within it the principle of the IALCs seeking funds direct from the wealthier parts of the Communion was well entrenched, and that of itself provided leverage to be brought to bear upon bishops across the Communion to help raise such funds.

Curiously, there was a further mention of IALCs in the resolutions, and that from an unexpected quarter, the apparently hostile Section 4. However, this resolution, which went through as uncontroversial, leaves it still marginally uncertain whether the liturgists are the policers or the policed:

'Resolution IV.12

Implications of Ecumenical Agreements

This Conference:
(a) encourages a fuller embodiment of the spirit and content of accepted agreed statements in the life and teaching of the Provinces; and
(b) urges that new Provincial liturgical texts and practices be consonant with accepted ecumenical agreements reached in multilateral and bilateral dialogues, for example BEM and ARCIC, and requests the Primates to consider appropriate ways for encouraging this in consultation with the International Anglican Liturgical Consultation.'

It is unclear whether anything of note has ever emerged from a Primates' meeting in relation to this resolution.

11. The Consultation that was not – Kottayam, 1999

The Steering Committee met at St Matthew's, Westminster, in London on 8-10 July 1998 just before the beginning of the Lambeth Conference, and drew up plans for Kottayam in 1999, noting that they had good prospects of offering 'bursary' funding to assist people attending from developing countries.[49] The Järvenpää papers were now in print, and the topic looked timely, as various Provinces were beginning to revise their Ordinals. Going to South India was a new venture by *Societas*, but one which the Steering Committee was glad to follow, reckoning it might bring a different balance of participants from that which meetings in Europe and North America had drawn. Letters went out; bursaries were offered; expectations were high.

Then a totally non-liturgical saga overtook the programme. India provides special conference visas for people to attend international conferences which have been registered with the immigration authorities. Registering was in the hands of the local Indians, and it appears that *Societas* was registered, but, through inadvertence or misunderstanding, IALC was not. As IALC preceded *Societas* on this occasion, those applying round the world for visas, whether they were staying to *Societas* or not, naturally sought conference visas and naturally put in IALC as the conference they were attending. Ron Dowling applied first himself, and was duly granted a visa (he later came to think that, after the then recent murder of Australian missionaries in India, the Indian consulate in Perth was keen to help Australians). This, however, proved not to be the case in the rest of the world, and in various places those who applied for a conference visa for IALC were not only informed that there was no such conference registered but also came under suspicion if, having been rejected under the conference heading, they then immediately applied for tourist visas. It is likely that the General Election due in India in September 1999 increased this sense of vigilance in embassies and consulates.[50] The upshot was that there arrived in Kottayam simply a somewhat random collection of persons who had either cited *Societas*, or found some other way into gaining a visa. Many who had been invited from Africa and elsewhere on bursaries were missing, in some cases after air fares had been purchased. A notable exception was David Gitari from Kenya who duly showed up.

---

[49] From most parts of the world fares to reach South India were high; but this factor was likely to be balanced by a cost of living in the country which was unbelievably cheap by Western standards.

[50] Thus in London Colin Buchanan only got his visa by asking for intervention by Lambeth Palace.

The Steering Committee had to face this situation when they convened (without Solomon Amusan) to do their preparation in the days before the Consultation began. They were were staying for two nights at the Hotel Green Park, next door to the Indian seminary (SEERI) where IALC was to meet. However, the problem proved to be far greater than simply the absence of some valued liturgists. Ron Dowling as chair was at the centre of events, and the crucial part of his own account reads as follows:

'On the evening before we were due to begin we were making the final arrangements when I was summoned to the door because two members of the local police were asking to see the convenor/chairman. They asked for my passport and looked at the visa. Then they insisted that I accompany them to the local police station with my passport. One of the CSI archdeacons also came with me (this seemed to have been pre-arranged on reflection). I was put in a room with an overhead fan and tall Indian officers at the door. The archdeacon went into the office of the police chief (whom I was told was a Christian) and there I sat for two or more hours. I remember thinking that it was like something out of a Humphrey Bogart movie, except it was actually happening to me. Eventually I was summoned in and told that our meeting was illegal and could not take place. This was an order from the government in Delhi. I was presented with a letter telling me this. My passport was returned to me and eventually I returned to the Hotel Green Park (where I was staying) to be greeted by a very anxious Steering Committee. What to do now? We would meet first thing the next morning. I did not sleep very much that night!

The meeting the following morning was attended by Fr Jacob Thekeparampil (SEERI), Dr Pulicken (owner of the Hotel Green Park), the manager of the hotel, myself and other members of the Steering Committee. Because the official letter banned a meeting of IALC at SEERI chaired by me, it was agreed by the Indian contingent that a meeting could be held at the Hotel Green Park (next door to SEERI – where many of us were staying), not called IALC and best not chaired by me. This idea was accepted, and the meeting, due to begin that afternoon, was transferred to the Hotel Green Park. This included all the meals. The necessary arrangements were made at the same costs as the meeting at SEERI.

At the opening gathering of the group that evening, I explained the situation as best I could, suggested we call ourselves "The Compass Rose Liturgical Touring Group"(!), and said that I would step aside as chair of the meeting and other members of the Steering Committee would chair various sessions. This was agreed to... '

The Steering Committee reckoned not only that the actual meeting of those coming to Kottayam must be informal, but also, through its somewhat unrepresentative character, should be dubbed no more than an 'interim' conference, with a full Consultation thus delayed until 2001. There was some slight embarrassment, in that the Steering Committee were apparently giving themselves another two years in office, but it was clearly impossible to complete the work on ordination liturgies (and kindred issues) in Kottayam with the somewhat random set of participants who had actually come – and it would have been unconstitutional to change the Steering Committee at such a meeting. For the four days of gathering there was plenty of group work to be addressed, and in the process some issues were identified more clearly, but the culmination of the work begun in Järvenpää was now postponed till 2001. Some preliminary drafting tasks were allocated to two or three persons from each group with a view to 2001, but the sustaining of international communication needed to make progress proved difficult, and little actual interaction occurred.

It was a relief to discover that the financial outcome was not as disastrous as the Steering Committee had feared. Some airline tickets for folk who did not come had in fact never been bought, and others qualified for a refund; so the Steering Committee retained a moderate bursary fund, though one which they still hoped to swell somewhat before offering renewed grants to invited participants in 2001.

Memories of Kottayam are, almost by definition, not particularly about liturgy.[51] But a meeting of the Steering Committee was planned for May 2000 in Toronto, with the actual Consultation to be in California in August 2001 when the ordination issues were finally to be addressed.

When ACC-11 met at Dundee in September 1999, Paul Gibson, now retired from his position as liturgical officer of the Anglican Church of Canada, but retaining in a voluntary capacity his role as the ACC's Co-ordinator for Liturgy, had provided in advance a brief report of what was planned for Kottayam, and this is published in the ACC's report.[52]

[51]   There were some further ripples, as local Christians evinced concern as to whether an anti-Christian bias was not being manifested by the BJP (Hindu Nationalist) government (especially with an election due imminently); and an American participant, Robert Brooks, was involved in prompting some discreet further enquires by the USA embassy in Delhi about religious freedom.
[52]   James M. Rosenthal and Margaret Rodgers (compilers), *The Communion We Share: Anglican Consultative Council XI, Scotland* (Morehouse Publishing, Harrisburg, 2000) pp.143-146. Paul Gibson was also asked to be Chaplain to the meeting (*id.* p. 16)

12. IALC-6, Berkeley, 2001

A new millennium had an element of a new start. It was not only that the Steering Committee now looked to a new IALC-6 to achieve what had not been possible in India. It was also that with the lapse of time there had been a passing away. In the late 1990s and into the early 2000s there died: Freddie Amoore, Laurie Bartlett, Evan Burge, Brian Davis, Eugene Fairweather, Tom Talley and Michael Vasey. Each of these seven was a significant theologian or practitioner in one of six different countries (Laurie Bartlett and Evan Burge both being Australians).[53] The Steering Committee in May 2000, looking towards August 2001, recognized that little or no promising drafting had arisen from the Kottayam event, and that a new start was needed. They specifically asked Ruth Meyers, David Holeton and Bill Crockett to do a draft document on orders and ordination.

Societas this time was meeting at Santa Clara near to San Francisco, so it was natural for the Steering Committee to look for a venue towards Louis Weil, a founder-member of the Consultations and professor of liturgy at the Church Divinity School of the Pacific (CDSP) in Berkeley, across the bay from San Francisco. Through his hospitality IALC-6 duly met at CDSP from 6 to 11 August 2001, using student halls of residence at the University of California in Berkeley. 73 persons participated, a record attendance in itself, and providing the fullest coverage of the nations of the world and of the extent of the Anglican Communion which had been achieved by any Consultation up to that point (including, for instance, persons from 10 provinces in Africa). Robert Gribben from the Uniting Church of Australia was now the ecumenical partner.

The preparation was well rewarded in the event. A major statement, 'To Equip the Saints', was agreed by the Consultation. It begins from 'The foundation of the life and ministry of the church is...baptism'; and this sets the whole range of ordination questions within what is now popularly called a 'baptismal ecclesiology'. Ordination is a function of the church, for the church, within the church (though always in the name of the Father, the Son and the Holy Spirit). Within the three inherited orders, the ministry of deacons varies through the various provinces, though a move exists towards a more widespread encouragement of 'vocational' deacons. Presbyters are presbyters rather than priests. It is worth examining whether they may not become presbyters by 'direct ordination' – certainly it is their

---

[53] Brian Davis and Michael Vasey died in middle age, the others past their threescore years and ten.

baptism which is the basis of their vocation to 'serve', rather than any necessary inbuilt character of deacon's orders. Bishops are to exercise their ministry unprelatically and for the building up of the Christian community. Much of the statement is then devoted to the actual ritual of ordination. The baptismal ecclesiology should undergird the whole rite. The laying on of hands with prayer should be absolutely central and not be overlaid or threatened by the burgeoning of secondary ceremonies. Richard Leggett from Canada was invited to contribute an appendix which cross-references the points of principle to statements in major ecumenical agreements of the previous three decades.

The statement was published as Paul Gibson (ed), *Anglican Ordination Rites* (Grove Worship Series 168, 2002). There is already evidence, as shown in the Introduction on page 4 above, that it has impacted actual liturgical revision almost immediately. As with the previous two statements, there then followed a major set of essays upon the statement, Ronald Dowling and David Holeton (eds), *Equipping the Saints: Ordination in Anglicanism Today* (Columba, Dublin, 2006).

The Berkeley Consultation in passing addressed a completely different issue which was affecting the Communion. Paul Gibson introduced a paper on 'Eucharistic Food – May We Substitute?' asking what breadth of interpretation might be allowed in the provision of sacramental food and drink. The Consultation asked the Standing Committee of the ACC to conduct a survey 'to determine practice in relation to the elements of holy communion throughout the Communion', with the proposal that the ACC form a working group, including IALC persons, to implement this. The ACC Standing Committee did not initially address this, but in December 2001 the Berkeley agenda came before the new post-Lambeth Commission, the Inter-Anglican Standing Commission on Ecumenical Relations (IASCER), which has responsibility for Anglican theological coherence worldwide. Bill Crockett, a regular member of IALCs, was also a member of IASCER, specifically as a consultant representing the concerns of the IALCs. The meeting already had ordination questions to handle in an ecumenical context; but the issue of the eucharistic elements came up unexpectedly at the meeting – and in the event IASCER in a statement entitled 'Eucharistic Food' proved cautious to the point of immovability on this issue, citing 'the Church's constant tradition'.

At the end of the Consultation, the periods of office on the Steering Committee of Ron Dowling, Solomon Amusan and Colin Buchanan all ceased. Sister Jean survived as she had the highest vote in 1995, and she was joined by Paul Bradshaw (England), who had the largest number of votes, and therefore was chartered to be a member for two Consultations, and by Joyce Karuri (Kenya) and Tomas Maddela (Philippines) to form the new Steering Committee, in which Ellison Pogo continued as the Primates' link. The Steering Committee in turn chose Paul Bradshaw to chair them for the coming four years.

Paul Gibson reported on Berkeley to ACC-12, meeting in Hong Kong in September 2002. The ACC took the issue of eucharistic elements more seriously than the statement on ordinations, and passed this resolution:

> 'Resolution 16: Inter Anglican Liturgical Consultation
> This Anglican Consultative Council:
> 1. awaits a survey by the Inter Anglican Liturgical Consultation of practice in relation to the elements of Holy Communion in the churches of the Anglican Communion, and of the reasons given for any departure from dominical command; and
> 2. requests that the results of such a survey be presented to the Joint Standing Committee upon completion.'[54]

This resolution gave impetus to a survey, which Paul Gibson himself then initiated.

Following that ACC meeting, IASCER met in December 2002 and this time engaged in depth with the Berkeley Statement on ordination. Bill Crockett responded on behalf of IALC to the questions raised, and later produced a consolidated written report on the dialogue for IALC members.

---

[54] 'Report of the Co-ordinator for Liturgy' in James Rosenthal (compiler), *For the Life of the World: The Official Report of the 12ᵗʰ Meeting of the Anglican Consultative Council, Hong Kong 2002* (Morehouse, Harrisburg, 2003) pp.393-397. In Resolution 16 cited here the printed title 'Inter Anglican...' appears to be an editorial error.

13. Interim Conference, Cuddesdon, 2003 and IALC-7, Prague, 2005

In 2003 *Societas* was scheduled to meet at Eindhoven in the Netherlands. The Steering Committee for reasons of cost and convenience, decided to hold the projected 'interim' conference in England just before the *Societas* Congress. The chosen venue was the premises of Ripon College, Cuddesdon (though a few participants had to be accommodated at St Stephen's House in Oxford, with transport provided each day). The conference was to run from 4 to 9 August, and the chosen topic was 'Liturgical Education and Formation'. 61 persons booked in, 28 from Europe, 14 from the USA and Canada (including Alan Detscher, a Roman Catholic liturgist from Connecticut, the ecumenical partner), 6 from Australia and New Zealand, 3 from South Africa and 10 from the rest of the world. Paul Bradshaw explained at the outset that it was an open question as to whether the theme would prove to be the gateway into the topic of the full Consultation planned for 2005, or whether it would in fact be a 'one-off', with another topic overtaking it in 2005. Seven papers were given, a notable opening one by Juan Oliver from Long Island, New York, on 'The meaning of liturgical formation'. Others, all on the stated topic, included Solomon Amusan of Nigeria 'from an African perspective' and Tomas Maddela from the Philippines on 'in ordination training'. There was plenary discussion and vigorous group work, along with the now normal reports from provinces. The final verdict of the Steering Committee, which had the benefit of evaluation sheets from the participants, was that the papers might well merit publication, and they were partly edited in preparation, but have not at the time of writing found a publisher. The Steering Committee also concluded that the 2005 Consultation need not address the same topic, and the Cuddesdon Conference passed into history as indeed a 'one-off' consideration.

At Cuddesdon Bill Crockett provided a full written report on both the IASCER meetings. In relation to the eucharistic elements, the Steering Committee then set up a small 'task force' of Ron Dowling (convenor), Ian Paton (Scotland), and Cynthia Botha (Southern Africa), and they went to work over the next two years to further the survey of actual practice in the Communion, reflect on the implications, and report back to IALC-7 in Prague.

A small but perhaps seminal innovation occurred the following year. Trevor Lloyd sounded out British and Irish participants in the conference in

August 2004 of the Society for Liturgical Study (SLS) to see whether there would be value in a 'regional' quasi-IALC 'informal gathering'. SLS is itself interdenominational and its members were coming to Mirfield from all parts of Britain and Ireland. Paul Gibson came also, and a total of 16 Anglicans stayed on for 24 hours after SLS to address IALC topics. Hard work in both groups and plenary provided statements on eucharistic elements, on 'commonality' of Anglican liturgical identity, and on some basic principles of pastoral rites. There was also, as at the international gatherings, some sharing of news from the different provinces. While the gathering came too late to be of direct use to the Steering Committee, which had already met to plan for the Prague Consultation, the participants at the very least prepared themselves for the Prague agenda, and their statements remained helpfully on record.

For 2005, *Societas* was to hold its Congress in Dresden, which is near to the border with the Czech Republic. This led to approaches to David Holeton to see whether IALC-7 could be held in Prague prior to the *Societas* week, and he was able to find appropriate acommodation at the Baptist seminary there. The Steering Committee decided for a topic on 'Liturgy and Anglican Identity', and both commissioned preparatory papers and built into the Consultation papers by Cynthia Botha, Trevor Lloyd and Louis Weil, with an ecumenical contribution made by John Melloh, a Roman Catholic from Notre Dame University, Indiana. 57 persons came, but the spread across the world was far more uneven than had been hoped. There was no-one from South America, or India, and, although the Pacific (not least Japan) had a sprinkling of participants, there were only three from Africa north of the Zambezi – alongside 22 from Britain and Ireland and 13 from North America. There were bursary funds to spare, but many provinces to which they were offered proved unable to use them.

Reports from different provinces occurred as usual, and Bill Crockett gave a full account of the IASCER meetings. The most recent one had been recommending guidelines for ecumenical participation in ordinations. The IALC task force on eucharistic elements now provided its report 'Eucharistic Food and Drink'; and their report revealed a wider spread of variations than IASCER was likely on previous form to approve. The Consultation was minded to affirm a norm and yet be wholly tolerant of variants. The report itself was now to be remitted to the ACC in accordance with their resolution of 2002. Thereafter it would be at the discretion of the ACC to disseminate, and the task force members were to remain in contact with each other with a view to possible revision of the document in the light of discussion. IASCER met in December 2005 and received the report 'with gratitude' and with acknowledgment of the 'substantial research' that had gone into it, but also reaffirmed its own conservative stance of 2001.

The main theme of liturgical identity proved slightly slippery to handle in the group discussion and did not lead to as weighty a statement as had emerged from most previous full Consultations. Instead the Consultation finished with a more provisional statement, exploring rather than asserting its theme 'Liturgy and Anglican Identity'. This was duplicated for the various provinces with a request for reactions to it. However, three of the main addresses were accepted for inclusion in the projected Alcuin/GROW Joint Liturgical Study 65, to be edited with a substantial introduction by Paul Bradshaw under the same title, *Liturgy and Anglican Identity*, in June 2008, and it was hoped the Prague Statement mentioned above would be included.

A new Steering Committee was to be appointed, with hopes expressed in the plenary meeting that the next full Consultation, IALC-8, could come after two years only, rather than four. George Connor (Aotearoa)(who received the most support and therefore serves two terms), Ian Paton (Scotland), and Cynthia Botha (Southern Africa) were appointed to join Paul Bradshaw on the Steering Committee. Paul Bradshaw continued as chair, and the Steering Committee decided at their meeting in 2006 that the Palermo gathering in 2007 would indeed be a full Consultation.

Meanwhile the Prague Statement itself went beyond circulation in duplicated form, as it was published in *Anglican World* no. 120 in New Year 2005/6. In summary, while the unity of the Anglican Communion was coming under vast pressures on other fronts, the role of liturgy – both its content and its ethos - in holding Anglicans together across the globe was being studied sympathetically and peaceably.

As this Study goes to press, preparations are well under way for IALC-8, to be held in Palermo, Sicily, from 30 July to 4 August 2007. The principal subject of the meeting will be funeral liturgies (probably as the first of a series of consultations addressing pastoral rites). The issues will be considered from historical/anthropological and cross-cultural points of view as well as from liturgical and theological perspectives. The pattern of working, the funding and the organizing seem now to be sufficiently assured to give good hopes of a future far beyond 2007.

'WHAT THE LAMBETH CONFERENCE DID NOT SAY ON LITURGY' [1998]
THE BUTCHERED DRAFT APPENDIX
to the Statement of Section 3 ('Called to be a faithful church in a plural world')

APPENDIX: CURRENT ANGLICAN CONCERNS IN LITURGY

Introduction
Paragraphs 2.32-2.35 within the main Statement above set out briefly some basic liturgical principles which have led us into a more detailed treatment here of specific matters on the liturgical agenda. Standing by those paragraphs of the Statement, we here affirm those same principles and, if the paragraphs had appeared here, they would have been headed 'Theology, Worship and Prayer in a Plural Church and World'. They are the backdrop to all which follows here.

2. The Unity of Anglicanism
Whilst this Conference addresses 'instruments of unity' in the Communion, we record a deeper bond of unity in our common historical roots and treasured liturgical tradition. This tradition was until recently embodied in the seventeenth century Prayer Books (with minor revisions in the first half of the present century) ; and these were central to the evolution of the Communion and placed a common experience of worship at its heart. But since the 1958 Lambeth Conference first gave guidance about liturgical revision, many Provinces have expanded and changed the received tradition, creating new texts alongside the old Prayer Books. Thus the earlier uniformity has given way to an ever-growing diversity. The new liturgical compilations not only use contemporary language, but also offer great diversity within and between Provinces, great flexibility in actual rites, and great scope to create liturgical forms which are true to each local culture – a process also reflected in music, ceremonial, architecture and ornamentation. Securing a true local identity may weaken family relationships between Provinces and may appear to imperil the identity of global Anglicanism.

Such worldwide concerns are now expressed and handled through the network known as the International Anglican Liturgical Consultations (IALCSs).* The 1988 Lambeth Conference came at the very point where the (informally convened) IALCs, which had already then met twice, had petitioned the ACC for some official recognition and support from the Communion. The ACC Executive Committee gave that recognition and, at IALC-3 at York in 1989, the relationship was accepted and recognized. It was later endorsed by the joint meeting of the Primates and ACC at Cape Town in January 1993.** The successive Consultations of 1989, 1991 and 1995, with more informal conferences at intervening times, have included an expanding participation by liturgists and other leaders of the Provinces, and have produced substantial statements and publications to help guide liturgical revision and creativity within the Provinces and to strengthen bonds between them.***

In relation to the bonds uniting the Communion, IALC-5 (held at Dublin to consider the eucharist in 1995) made the following statement: 'In the future, Anglican unity will find its liturgical expression not so much in uniform texts and ceremonies...as in a common approach to eucharistic celebration and a structure which will ensure a balance of word, prayer and sacrament...' We believe the issue of a common identity to our worldwide Communion will be resolved in line with this statement; but it implicitly places greater responsibility on bishops and other leaders and teachers of liturgy to understand those historical structures and to provide the Provinces with appropriate educational resources.

3. Baptism
The 1988 Lambeth Conference report treated baptism at length in the section report of 'Mission and Ministry'; and IALC-4 on initiation at Toronto in 1991 followed it up with weighty recommendations. Bishops at Lambeth and liturgists at Toronto agreed that water-baptism is the sacrament of initiation, that it provides complete sacramental initiation given once-for-life. It is properly given to infants and children in appropriate Christian contexts, and, where this is so, then the theology and ritual of baptism must be as\far as possible common to adults and to infants and to all intermediate ages, a commonality which should be expressed by a common liturgical order, irrespective of the age of the candidates. From these assertions we draw the following implications:
- Baptism is God's charter for mission [concerning which see paras xx-xx].
- Baptism formally admits to holy communion, so the onus of proof lies upon any who would delay baptism until the baptized have fulfilled further qualifications.
- Confirmation stands as a pastoral office, and this raises a question as to how far it should be treated as a Part of initiation. It is appropriate for the personal affirmation of baptismal vows for those baptized as infants and now come of age, and it is valued by bishops and candidates alike for the pastoral role the bishop thus fulfils towards the laity of the diocese; but it is less appropriate for receiving baptized Christians from other denominations or for adding after the baptism of a adult, and such practices should be radically re-examined.
- We commend developing pattern for an adult catechumenate in preparation for baptism, confirmation, or restoration of the lapsed. The role of adult sponsors of candidates leads to growth and unity in Christ for all concerned.
- Nothing should be allowed to undermine the given-ness and validity of infant baptism; but we see a pastoral need for ways of restoring the lapsed, and would encourage Provinces to explore such possibilities creatively.
- In the conduct of baptisms, we welcome the use, in appropriate contexts, of submersion; we judge the use of water with 'the Name of the Father, the Son and the Holy Spirit' to be non-negotiable; and we believe that the normal context ought to be the main public worship of the local church with as full a congregation as possible.

4. Eucharist

IALC-5 at Dublin in 1995 adopted Principles and Recommendations which we now commend to the Provinces of the Anglican Communion. From this report we draw attention to the following specific points:

- the eucharist is in principle the defining event of corporate worship;
- the structure of the eucharist includes a gathering of the people of God, a full and indispensable ministry of the word, a provision for prayers of thanksgiving and intercession, a liturgy of the sacrament, introduced by a sharing of the Peace and carried through with a responsive eucharistic prayer and distribution in both kinds, and a dismissal;
- the eucharistic prayer ideally includes our giving 'thanks and praise' for God's acts in creation and salvation, a citing of the account of our Lords institution of the sacrament as the warrant for our contemporary celebration of the Supper and a prayer for the participation in communion to transform the communicants, which is the work of the Holy Spirit. The whole eucharistic prayer ought to be viewed as consecratory, and this puts in question the appropriateness of any action or ceremonial which would suggest that one phrase or sentence in it is a special point of consecration.
- the whole congregation celebrates the sacrament together, and, although the presidential role includes articulation of the eucharistic prayer, this prayer too is the prayer of the whole people. The issue of whether a lay person may preside is raised in section 5 below.
- the rite should reflect the context and culture of the people where it is celebrated. We refer to general principles of inculturation in section 8 below, including the handling of a specific sensitive case referred to us.

5. Diverse Ministries in One Church

Christ alone is our high priest; the people of God have a derived priesthood of worship and service; and within that priesthood chosen persons are are called to specific ministries of leadership in mission and of pastoral and liturgical care. It is the task of ordination rites not only to ordain to specific orders, but to set out clearly the ministry be exercised within each of those orders. A detailed discussion of the roles of deacon and of bishop is to be found in [draft delivered to us].

'Orders' are not qualities inserted into the persons who are ordained; rather they are a feature of the structuring of the church on earth into which the persons are inserted. Thus ordination is not so much the conferring of powers of functions by a bishop onto a candidate as it is the church adding to the ranks of its ministers within a certain order. The participation of the community is this integral to the act of ordination, in the acclamatory assent and in the prayers. The bishop's prayer and the laying on of hands are central but are not disconnected from the part of the people. In the Jarvenpaa conference mentioned below Paul Bradshaw expressed this ecclesiology this way: 'Prayer by the assembled community is not a mere preliminary to the "real thing", but as much part of the "form" of ordination as the ordination prayer itself...It should be introduced by an appropriately worded bidding that expresses the theological conviction that ordination is an act of God working through the whole Church and not just through the bishop alone.'****

The IALC held an 'interim' Conference on orders and ordination at Jarvenpaa in Finland in 1997, and this ecclesiology informed the whole work of the Conference. The published papers and findings demonstrate how the question of the relation of orders to the whole people of God has surfaced strongly, and with it the question of how the baptismal call to service of that whole people can best be expressed within the rites which call specific people into particular orders for more carefully identified lives of leadership and service within the whole people.

Earlier the Dublin Consultation (see p... above) addressed the question of possible lay presidency of the eucharist, a question raised in several parts of the world. Without suggesting a definitive resolution of the issue, the Consultation adopted this guiding principle 'The liturgical functions of the ordained arise out of pastoral responsibility. Separating liturgical functions and pastoral oversight tends to reduce liturgical presidemcy to an isolated ritual function.' We suggest that careful reflection on this point should accompany any wrestling with the question of lay presidency, which is treated also at para 3.24 in the main Statement.

6. Commemoration of Saints in the Calendar

The 1988 Lambeth Conference, on the proposal of the African Provinces that the Anglican Communion should recognize as saints men and women who have lived godly lives, in resolution 60 asked the ACC to take the matter further. The ACC duly asked the Co-ordinator for Liturgy to prepare suitable guidelines, taking the advice of the IALC and earlier documentation into account. He then produced draft guidelines and the ACC at Cape Town in 1993 adopted these as appropriately expressing principles and criteria for the recognition of those who have led holy lives. Such recognition has to begin where they lived, even if it spreads to all the world. The guidelines are appended to the Cape Town report, and should be consulted whenever such a progress is in view.

7. Diversity of Texts and the Technological Revolution

As immense changes occur through liturgical revision and enrichment, and as these differ greatly from Province to Province, and differ within Provinces as to their status and authority, so the technological revolution both assists in the multiplication process on the one hand, but offers the opportunity of easy storage, retrieval and cross-fertilization on the other. Whilst in some parts of the world books are an expensive luxury, and it would be wasteful to replace books which still have life in them, in other parts printed Prayer Books are being supplemented and supplanted in use by the role of electronic technology.

8. Inculturation

The 1988 Lambeth resolutions included two (nos.22 and 47) which affirmed the importance of inculturation of the liturgy and urged individual Provinces to see themselves as free, subject to 'essential Anglican universal norms of worship' and to a valuing of traditional liturgical materials, to seek that expression of worship which is appropriate to its Christian people in their cultural context. The 1989 York Consultation (IALC3) identified the incarnation as God's self-inculturation in this world and in a particular context; and we are wise to follow that model. It would involve the forms of expression of the liturgy growing fro within their local cultures as naturally as Christian forms first grew within and from the context of Jewish liturgy.

The history of Anglicanism become global is a story weak on inculturation. Certainly the use of vernacular languages in every part of the world has been axiomatic from the earliest point, but at almost every other point the liturgical cultures of England have been dominant. The York Consultation noted the need to keep the following areas under close scrutiny: language forms, music, architecture, ceremonies, sacramental elements, rites of passage, the relationship between liturgy and identification with the oppressed, and agape meals. As a general rule in the Communion it is only in very recent years that there have been serious signs of European ways giving place to more local expressions. Even then, we share the caution of those who, through illiteracy or difficulty with the printed word, are in particular pastoral need of the conserving and continued repetition of the familiar forms – whether as spoken text or the words of songs and hymns. With that caution we rejoice at every sign of progress achieved in implementing true inculturation since the resolutions of the last Lambeth Conference, and reaffirm its continued validity and urgency.

One particular instance of the tension described earlier between the liturgical expression of the culture and the worldwide unity of the whole church has emerged strongly at this Lambeth. It concerns the sensitive issue of the sacramental elements at holy communion. On the one hand there is an almost unbroken universal practice of nearly two thousand years of celebrating communion with wheat-bread and grape-wine; on the other we have heard compelling pleas (including the findings of the pan-African Kanamai Consultation and IALC-5 in Dublin) that in some parts of the world these forms of food and drink may well be culturally alien or prohibitively expensive or both, and that the traditional practice is therefore to be severely questioned. Our own recommendation is that in cases of great necessity individual Provinces should be free to permit particular dioceses or areas to vary the traditional uses under carefully controlled conditions and with a view to the local authenticity and biblical credibility of the elements thus permitted.

Full attention to the issues of daily life in the pattern of any culture must include attention to Christian worship in the context of that culture as well. Inculturated worship is no substitute for integrity in social relationships, but will provide a graceful model. As IALC-3 at York observed, 'The liturgy, rightly constructed, forms the people of God, enabling them for their mission of evangelism and social justice in their culture and society.'

---

*   [The original footnote summarized the history of IALCs to that point, set out more fully in this Study]

**   [Original footnote] It is important to note that in 1989 the Anglican Church of Canada seconded their liturgical officer, the Rev. Paul Gibson, to work on a part-time basis as Co-ordinator for Liturgy to the Communion; and his work, through the request of the Cape Town meeting, has facilitated the work of the IALCs and become almost indispensable to them. His recent report submitted to the ACC is appended to the Lambeth Report (see p... below). We note with concern that his retirement from the secondment work is due in 1999.

***   [The original footnote listed the dates of the actual Consultations and intermediate Conferences with information about their publications]

****   [Original footnote] Paul Bradshaw, 'Ordination as God's Action through the Church' in David R. Holeton (ed), *Anglican Orders and Ordinations* (Alcuin/GROW Joint Liturgical Study no.39, Grove Books Ltd, 1997) p.10.

Editorial note in 1998: Colin Buchanan added this note in the reprint of the blocked draft in *News of Liturgy* in September 1998:

> *Warning*: Note that, despite the drafted text, there is no guarantee that anything particular will appear in the final version of the [Section's] Statement and, equally, no guarantee that the 'Report of the Co-ordinator for Liturgy' will be printed with the Lambeth Statement – indeed it seems probable it will not.

Editorial note in 2007: The draft as printed in NOL had been left unpolished and has all the marks of its working draft status upon it. At the time the draft was thus published unofficially, the main Statement was undergoing a smoothing editorial process, and it was unknown how it would emerge, though Colin Buchanan entertained some faint hope that in some way it would include the above material. In the event it did not, nor was Paul Gibson's report in it. The Section 3 report is by far the shortest of the four Section Reports, and it is hard now to see even the supposed points of contact anticipated by the first line of the draft. There are slight passing references to liturgy on pages 192-3 of the full 1998 Lambeth Conference Report, and that is all.